Searching for Eden

MERCER
UNIVERSITY PRESS

Endowed by

TOM WATSON BROWN

and

THE WATSON-BROWN FOUNDATION, INC.

Searching for Eden

John Steinbeck's Ethical Career

JOHN H. TIMMERMAN

MERCER UNIVERSITY PRESS
MACON, GEORGIA

MUP/ H885

Published by Mercer University Press, Macon, Georgia 31207

1400 Coleman Avenue
Macon, Georgia 31207

9 8 7 6 5 4 3 2 1

Books published by Mercer University Press are printed on acid-free paper that meets the requirements of the American National Standard for Information Sciences—Permanence of Paper for Printed Library Materials.

Library of Congress Cataloging-in-Publication Data

Timmerman, John H.
Searching for Eden : John Steinbeck's Ethical Career / John H. Timmerman. -- First edition.
pages cm
Includes bibliographical references and index.
ISBN-13: 978-0-88146-478-8 (hardback : acid-free paper)
ISBN-10: 0-88146-478-3 (hardback : acid-free paper)
1. Steinbeck, John, 1902-1968--Criticism and interpretation. 2. Steinbeck, John, 1902-1968--Ethics. 3. Moral conditions in literature. I. Title.
PS3537.T3234Z9284 2014
813'.52--dc23

2014000362

Contents

Acknowledgments

Special permissions requested and received to quote passages from works by Steinbeck include the following:

From *The Acts of King Arthur and his Noble Knights* by John Steinbeck, edited by Chase Horton, copyright © 1976 by Elaine Steinbeck. Used by permission of Viking Penguin, a division of Penguin Group (USA) LLC.

From *The Grapes of Wrath* by John Steinbeck, copyright 1939, renewed © 1967 by John Steinbeck. Used by permission of Viking Penguin, a division of Penguin Group (USA) LLC.

From *The Pearl,* by John Steinbeck. Copyright 1945 by John Steinbeck, renewed © 1973 by Elaine Steinbeck, John Steinbeck IV, and Thom Steinbeck. Used by permission of Viking Penguin, a division of Penguin Group (USA) LLC.

From *The Log from the Sea of Cortez,* by John Steinbeck, copyright 1941 by John Steinbeck and Edward F. Ricketts. Copyright renewed ©1969 by John Steinbeck and Edward F. Ricketts Jr. Copyright (c) 1951 by John Steinbeck. Copyright renewed (c) 1975 by Elaine Steinbeck, John Steinbeck IV and Thom Steinbeck. Used by permission of Viking Penguin, a division of Penguin Group (USA) LLC.

From *Travels with Charley,* by John Steinbeck. Copyright © 1961, 1962 by The Curtis Publishing Co., Inc. Copyright © 1962 by John Steinbeck, renewed (c) by Elaine Steinbeck, Thom Steinbeck, and John Steinbeck IV. Used by permission of Viking Penguin, a division of Penguin Group (USA), LLC.

From *East of Eden,* by John Steinbeck. Copyright 1952 by John Steinbeck, renewed © 1980 by Elaine Steinbeck, John Steinbeck IV, and Thom Steinbeck. Used by permission of Viking Penguin, a division of Penguin Group (USA) LLC.

From *Journal of a Novel: The* East of Eden *Letters,* by John Steinbeck. Copyright © 1969 by the Executors of the Estate of John Steinbeck. Used by permission of Viking Penguin, a division of Penguin Group (USA) LLC.

ABBREVIATIONS

For the reader's ease of reference, all quotations from the primary sources of Steinbeck's work are noted with page numbers parenthetically in the text. Listed in chronological order of original publication and with abbreviations used in the text, editions used for this study are as follows:

TF	*Tortilla Flat* (New York: Covici-Friede, 1935). The later Random House-Modern Library edition retains the same pagination.
IDB	*In Dubious Battle* (New York: Covici-Friede, 1936; New York: Penguin Books, 1979).
OMM	*Of Mice and Men* (New York: Covici-Friede, 1937).
GOW	*The Grapes of Wrath* (New York: Viking Press, 1939). The later Viking Critical Edition, ed. Peter Lisca, retains the same pagination.
CR	*Cannery Row* (New York: Viking Press, 1945).
Pearl	*The Pearl* (New York: Viking Press, 1947).
LSC	*The Log from the Sea of Cortez* (New York: Viking Press, 1951).
EOE	*East of Eden* (New York: Viking Press, 1952).
ST	*Sweet Thursday* (New York: Viking Press, 1954.
TRP	*The Red Pony* (New York: Viking Press 1959; reissue of the 1945 illustrated edition).
WOD	*The Winter of Our Discontent* (New York: Viking Press, 1961).
TWC	*Travels with Charley in Search of America* (New York: Viking Press, 1962).
JN	*Journal of a Novel: The East of Eden Letters* (New York: Viking Press, 1969).

LL	*Steinbeck: A Life in Letters*. Ed. Elaine Steinbeck and Robert Wallsten (New York: Viking Press, 1975).
ACTS	*The Acts of King Arthur and His Noble Knights* (New York: Viking Press, 1976).
DAYS	*Working Days: The Journals of* The Grapes of Wrath. Ed. Robert DeMott (New York: Viking Press, 1989).
AAA	*America and Americans and Selected Nonfiction*. Ed. Susan Shillinglaw and Jackson J. Benson (New York: Penguin Classics, 2003).

Introduction

That John Steinbeck has been called a prophet or adopted a prophetic voice in his later writings at least, is a proposition made so frequently that it has been robbed of meaning. In fact, in our age as in Steinbeck's the very term *prophet* is bereft of common understanding. Properly understood, the term combines two elemental concepts. The first is that the prophet is situated in his or her time, perceptively aware of both its need and moral indignities. At once, the prophet also functions as a visionary; that is, he is gifted with some divine means of discerning the people of his age situated at a future time, whether for good or evil. Summarily, he sees what must be done to fulfill the vision with consequent benefaction—or what must be avoided to escape condemnation. It is no wonder that the people of an age rejects its prophets; they want only the good news.

The paradox inherent in Steinbeck's work is that his readers, then as now, appreciate his prophetic voice when he fictionalized the bad news. He seemed always at his most powerful state, his clearest voice, his most perceptive vision when he dramatized the message—that the United States was a nation crying in need, that we have despoiled its riches, that we have abused then forgotten its needy. So too his reputation as a reformer was established, for every prophet who decries the present state of his people at the very least implies a means of rectifying that state. In all his traditional responses—the family of man, the necessity of helping those in need, the dignity of the individual—this was the prophetic task Steinbeck adopted.

For how long, however, can the prophet restrain himself when people cluck their tongues in sympathy, wag their heads, and go on to the next new novel? Does he adopt a different voice? Instead of dramatizing need so that people look upon it, does his voice grow shrill and direct, a siren warning of a way one should not go? Or, like Isaiah, does he adopt the voice of reason: "Come now, let us reason together" (Isa 1:18)? Perhaps the rational argument will persuade the court and jury to reasonable action. Or, does he disengage, packing his dog and his gear into a truck named *Rocinante* and leaving behind in miles traveled what he could never escape in his mind?

This is a book about one man in two quite different ethical stances in his life and his literary career during the years 1930 to 1965. The first of these may be called Social Justice; the second Ideal Justice. Essentially a naturalist in belief, a realist in style, and a parabolist in intention, Steinbeck would seem to be a difficult case for an ethical study.[1]

Over the course of his long career, ethics for Steinbeck always entailed social justice. Justice is constituted of a communal spirit, a relational situation in which humans care for their fellows, and a state that champions the cause of the needy and outcast. Any violation of this code constitutes an ethical wrong. That violation merits punishment if incurred by an individual or rebellion if incurred by the state. Unfortunately, the needy and outcast often lack the strength and resources to do either. In his fiction of the 1930s, then, Steinbeck exposes the needs of social outcasts and the lack of

---

[1] I use *parabolist* here to convey the full meaning of the Greek *parabole*: although frequently misunderstood simply as an earthly story with a religious or spiritual meaning, the Greek term literally means "to set side by side." Thus Steinbeck sets markers in his stories (symbols or images) that suggest some meaning left unstated but larger than the narrative account.

response to their need by what he often referred to in *Cannery Row* as the tyranny of "civilization."

Social justice further emerged during the 1940s, a time when Steinbeck's own metaphysical appraisal of the world underwent upheaval. Ethical wrongs became evil, and humanity itself seemed starved for some crumb of beneficence. The Arthurian Danny and the Boys from *Tortilla Flat* dissolve into the broken Siege of Mack in *Cannery Row*. Steinbeck's darkening vision through the 1940s alleviated only slowly with the decade's passing.

For Steinbeck, an ideal ethics emerged around 1950 and governed his thinking and prose until his death in 1968. Robert DeMott points out in *Steinbeck's Reading* that "Steinbeck moved increasingly from a communal vision of life toward an engagement with universal human values rooted in traditional notions of creative choice, individual consciousness and inherited legacy."[2] In effect, Steinbeck sought those truths and values, that sense of right and wrong, that have prevailed throughout western culture. Unlike social ethics, which are constructed on naturalistic premises, are pragmatic, and are democratic, ideal ethics arise from transcendent norms, deal with ideal values, and seek the best guides from past culture and mythology. That seeking turned Steinbeck simultaneously to fifteenth-century England and a ten-year enterprise of translating Malory, particularly the great Chivalric code, and also to his own twentieth-century America in an effort to distinguish where we have gone wrong and where right.

While in his earlier work it might be said that Steinbeck's ethical task was to expose need, he began to understand a deeper calling to locate ethical answers for that need. Three important cultural shifts in twentieth-century American history

---

[2] Robert DeMott, *Steinbeck's Reading: A Catalogue of Books Owned and Borrowed* (New York: Garland, 1984) xxxi.

affected Steinbeck's changing ethical views. First, the Great Depression made clear to him that the existential, self-pleasure principle of non-teleological thinking was deeply, profoundly flawed. With a concept appearing already in *The Grapes of Wrath,* Steinbeck held that humans have an ethical responsibility to help their fellows, or else an essential part of their humanity is twisted. This view receives its fullest treatment in *East of Eden* (1952). The second major event was the Vietnam War. Steinbeck himself went to Vietnam as a journalist, acquiring a firsthand experience of this war that he had already experienced as a journalist during WWII. War, he came to believe, is the ultimate degradation and cheapening of human life. The third event occurred with the civil rights struggles of the 1950s and 60s. Again, Steinbeck visited the scenes of conflict and wrote about them in his most straightforward ethical treatises, *Travels with Charley* and *America and Americans*.

In few places, however, does Steinbeck's increasing dependence on an ideal ethic become more clear than in his compelling absorption with *Morte D'Arthur*. When Steinbeck was nine years old, his aunt gave him a copy of Malory's *Morte D'Arthur* in translation. The great romance was never far from him after that, either personally or in his writing. Merlin appears as a character in his first published novel. Merlin also is included in the first chapter of *The Acts of King Arthur and his Noble Knights*. Steinbeck's third book, *Tortilla Flat,* features characters patterned after King Arthur and the Knights of the Round Table.

During approximately the last fifteen years of his life, Steinbeck worked on a translation of Malory from the Middle English into modern form. These years are to be the central focus of this study. His final, posthumous work, *The Acts of King Arthur and his Noble Knights,* departs from Malory's essential form, style, and Chivalric code. Nonetheless, Steinbeck used the work as an opportunity to confirm his own final ethical code for the mid-twentieth century. My overall intention in this study is to trace the development of Steinbeck's ethical views throughout his career, then to demonstrate the effects of Malory's ethical thought upon *Travels with Charley* and *America and Americans* as ethical documents.

If we hope to shape some understanding of Steinbeck's ethical thinking, then several paths have to converge in this study. First, we discover that Steinbeck's early ethical creeds, while often steeped in convoluted language and theory, are rather raw attempts to position humanity according to individual needs and biological determinism. In the middle phase, Steinbeck appeared to become more aware of evil as an agency, and that humanity had to undertake decisive commitments and actions to defeat this evil. Finally, we see in the third phase, here deemed contemporaneous with Steinbeck's labor on Malory, that humanity must develop a code of right action. This code is not simply individually efficacious or for expedient ends, but it does indeed answer to ethical demands of community and teleology.

1

Ethics and Actions

A multiplicity of terms related to ethical thinking has surfaced in the scholarship on Steinbeck's thought. "Virtues," "values," "moral views," and "ethics" seem to be used nearly interchangeably. While each may suggest similar things, each also bears distinct philosophical nuances. The situation grows further complicated by the fact that while Steinbeck always considered himself first and foremost a writer of fiction, one whose aims were to tell a good story and to keep the reader happy, he also considered himself a philosopher.

Indeed, from his study of marine biology and its philosophical implications to the extensive collection of philosophical works in his personal library, Steinbeck may legitimately be called an amateur philosopher, meaning one who loves philosophical inquiry. Necessarily, however, some definition of terms related to ethics and that will guide this study is necessary.

We begin, as with all philosophical sciences, with assumptions or presuppositions essential to this science of ethics. Primary among these is that humans are by nature social beings. There is an essential "likeness" that unifies us and that transcends any particular cultural or personal traits. Consequently, we observe that when one human acts, others are necessarily affected by what he or she does. One's choices have social consequences. Similarly, the community in which that person lives affects one's personal choices. Were there only one person on the face of the earth, one could hardly speak of his facing an ethical dilemma or of his having an ethical choice. All such terms would be rendered meaningless.

This assumption that all ethics is social should not be mistaken for naturalistic behaviorialism, the idea that we cannot escape the social values that have codified our life behavior. Essential to any ethics is the free choice of the individual. In fact, this further belief often motivates the transcendent ethics of many religions—the idea that an individual, guided by certain metaphysical stipulations, can cultivate a self-discipline and moral system unassuageable by social influences.

If the first assumption is that ethics takes shape in human community, the second is that only humans are ethical agents. Plants, rocks, the elements, are nonrational as they cannot choose. We may bear ethical responsibility *toward* animals, but they are incapable of bearing such toward us. Therefore, humans alone can stand in ethical tension. In fact, such moral tension and consequential ethical struggle are definitive of humanity alone. Humanity alone is the proper object of ethical study. Ethicist Henry Stob sharpens the point: "Ethics is focused upon the individual because only the individual is truly personal and therefore an authentic moral agent."[1] From our two primary assumptions, we conclude that the proper subject of ethical inquiry is how the individual human acts in society. Responsibility rests upon individuals, but, since no individual is discrete, he always stands relationally in a social context. Clearly, Steinbeck's stories posit just such situations. If, however, we can locate the assumptions of ethics and their conclusions, we must also consider several of their

[1] Henry Stob, *Ethical Reflections: Essays on Moral Themes* (Grand Rapids MI: Wm. B. Eerdmans, 1978) 11.

implications, for these too will shed considerable light on the shadowy nuances of Steinbeck's beliefs.

First among those implications is to distinguish between involuntary and voluntary actions. Even these are further distinguished, including non-voluntary acts such as responding to laws of physics or other conditions necessary for life itself. Involuntary actions are those we do without will or thought. We distinguished between animals and humanity, claiming that animals are not ethical beings, yet we share common involuntary actions with animals. Our hearts beat similarly, as do our lungs to draw air and our digestive tracts to draw nourishment.[2] Properly, neither involuntary nor non-voluntary acts are the subject of ethics. They respond to other scientific inquiry—physics or biology or anatomy, for example. Only voluntary acts, those determined by an act of the will—either under or capable of being under reason—are the purview of ethical inquiry. It should be readily apparent that what one does not do, or, choosing a non-active position, is also a voluntary act and subject to ethical evaluation. To choose against doing something is equally an act of will as choosing to do something.

While we necessarily begin with actions, since not all actions are voluntary or determined by will, the attendant question is whether humans have free choice to act. A choice is free if, and only if, it is between open alternatives. One may do this or do that only if there is no factor but choosing itself that

---

[2] The distinction dates in western philosophy to Aristotle, who argues the theory of predication. Thus we can predicate 'animal' of 'man' as one elementary category. The fullest expression of Aristotle's natural science occurs in *De Partibus Animalium.* The categories pose problems for contemporary ethicists. See Marc D. Hauser, *Moral Minds: How Nature Designed Our Universal Sense of Right and Wrong* (New York: HarperCollins, 2006) particularly in Part III, "Evolving Code."

settles which alternative is chosen. I may choose to be a blacksmith or a jet fighter pilot only if they are practical alternatives. If I have no arms, neither alternative is open to choice. If I have a fear of high speed and combat, only one choice is open, but then again I have no practical choice. As John Finnis wrote,

> Free choice can only be understood and affirmed by one who understands that the chooser really did confront what I have called *open alternatives*.... Free choice could not rationally be affirmed in anthropology or metaphysics were there not an experience of free choice. But that experience is not of something happening to oneself; rather it is the experience of doing something, i.e. of *praxis*. And in the first instance it is the experience of confronting alternatives grasped by practical understanding as goods.[3]

Finally, free choice is not momentary. I can choose to tip a waitress five dollars or ten dollars. While that choice does have consequences for the waitress, it is not a moral choice. It is a social recognition for the worth of a service rendered. All free choices last. They last most significantly in the person who makes them, but the community in which they are made. Something changes in free choice.

The second implication relevant to our investigation, then, is that ethics has to do with the activity of an individual human in social context that may be judged. Several qualifications, however, apply here. One person's activity, for example, may be observed. Tom saw a brown wallet on the floor and slipped it into his own pocket. This describes an action, but it is ambiguous. Was it his own wallet? Was it someone else's? What did he do with the wallet? Turn it in to some authority? Use the credit cards and spend the cash? None of these

---

[3] John Finnis, *Fundamentals of Ethics* (Washington DC: Georgetown University Press, 1983) 137–38.

questions are answered by the descriptive act. Furthermore, as Henry Stob has pointed out, one must distinguish "between *causes of* and *reasons for* human behavior."[4] The former is the subject of social sciences; the latter the subject of ethics. Behavioral determinism is transcended by a distinctively moral analysis that considers the action itself. Conduct is analyzed and judged not according to description or causal explanation but according to some transcendent norm or demand.

In the tradition of ethics many alternatives for this transcendent norm appear. The empiricist David Hume, for example, denied the presence of eternal laws for justice. Instead he argues that justice depends upon a "felt utility" for social organization.[5] While humanity feels the need for justice, reason organizes it into social rules. In Hume's process, it would be fair to say that we "feel" values, rather than deduce values rationally or arrive at them rationally from abstract principles. Finally, his ethics rest upon characters, not upon anything like a transcendent norm. This is especially evident in his distinction between virtue and vice as sentiments. Recognizing and acting upon the need of others produces happiness, and is therefore a virtue; ignoring such need represents a social wrong or vice.

Consider further Henry Stob's claim that *causes of* an action are not the proper subject of ethics, but rather of social sciences. A utilitarian, then, describes one *reason for* the way an individual acts. This view does indeed typify a number of characters, particularly in Steinbeck's early fiction. We call to mind, for example, *Tortilla Flat,* where to live happily is to live indeed. But that halcyon landscape darkens quickly in

---

[4] Stob, *Ethical Reflections,* 15.

[5] See David Hume, *Inquiry Concerning the Principles of Morals,* ed. L. A. Selby-Bigge (Oxford: Oxford University Press, 1902, 1951) particularly 3.2.1.

following works. One might suggest that utilitarian ethics are at work in *In Dubious Battle,* claiming that the telos of the actions are for the happiness and well being of the worker. If so, it is only under the clangor of clubs on bodies, guttering fires, and the cries of the disenfranchised. This is not utilitarian; it is warfare. So we have to ask more profound ethical questions: which side is just in the warfare? Is there an intrinsic good worth going to battle for?

In his study of utilitarian philosophy in Steinbeck's fiction, John J. Han lists the many ethical philosophies that have been attributed to Steinbeck but suggests that "Although he never identified any specific moral theory as his own, he lived in a culture heavily influenced by utilitarianism."[6] As Han applies his thesis, he argues that Steinbeck's fictional world is one of an Act Utilitarianism; that is, an act is not moral or immoral based upon the greatest good for the greatest number, but based upon its effect in a specific circumstance. If one distinguishes between the two great strands of ethics philosophy—theory and practice, thought ethics and applied—then Han's argument would situate Steinbeck on the practical and applied side. Most certainly this is the case in Steinbeck's early work, as we shall investigate in chapter 2. And, although he doesn't make this precise point, nearly all of Han's examples are drawn from the literature of the 1930s. But the do not necessarily apply for later time periods of Steinbeck's fiction career. What changes occurred to challenge Steinbeck's relativist ethics of utilitarianism? Was there a more coherent and muscular ethic he adopted instead? Certainly Han is correct to a degree. Steinbeck was not a reflective, theoretical ethicist. He wouldn't have considered himself an ethicist at all, yet these facts make

---

[6] John J. Han, "'I Want to Make 'Em Happy': Utilitarian Philosophy in John Steinbeck's Fiction," *The Moral Philosophy of John Steinbeck,* ed. Stephen K. George (Lanham MD: Scarecrow Press, 2005) 41.

all the more important an investigation into his views during the latter years of his life.

Then too, many normative characteristics of human experience, once highly valued, are not necessarily the subject of ethics. For example, we might argue that the primary characteristic of logic is consistency. Consistency then is its virtue as a philosophical science. Furthermore we might admire consistency in human character insofar as we understand it as dependability. We admire dependable people; we discount those who are undependable, yet consistency alone can hardly be construed as an ethical norm. After all, a serial killer might be consistent in his or her *modus operandi*. We speak often of consistency in the law as a good thing, yet the law itself, as we witness from endless debate or appeal, may be wrong or even evil.

What do these arguments have to teach us about ethics? First, ethics, the science of morality, is not concerned with every kind of judgment an individual *voluntarily* makes. One's decision to wear a suit or a pair of jeans is not a moral decision. One's decision to disrobe in public could be a moral decision if it brings offense to the social community. Second, ethics is concerned with moral judgment about the rightness or wrongness of conduct. Third, this judgment does not arise from a particular sentiment (one might be offended that another chose to wear jeans to a formal ball), but it arises from a norm or idea of the right or the good (although the empiricists argued otherwise). As such, ethics is not concerned with whether certain conduct is pleasurable, or even it if brings happiness, but only whether it conforms to a moral law or ideal. It is precisely such an ethic that operates in Steinbeck's later fiction. A character trespasses a moral norm and thereby both offends society and also diminishes his own human nature. The question remains, however, where such norms come from, how they are constituted, and what their effects are in regard to human behavior.

Melville and Steinbeck

As for the source of evil or sin itself, it is enlightening to view Steinbeck in the context of an earlier American author, Herman Melville, who himself struggled artistically with the "mystery of iniquity." A word of caution must be mentioned here, for it is difficult to determine how close Steinbeck's reading of Melville was. Robert DeMott has cited three references to Melville in *Steinbeck's Reading* and has thoroughly investigated influences of *Moby-Dick* on *East of Eden.*[7] On the other hand, we recognize that Melville was virtually the forgotten man of American letters until scholars started a revival of interest during the 1950s. The echoes of Melville's thought generally—and specifically the determinative nature of the sea and a subsequent naturalistic ethics—bears so many similarities to Steinbeck's own that it seems difficult to deny the influence or relationship. While Melville developed his ethics of good and evil throughout his life, it may be seen most effectively in his summary novella, *Billy Budd, Sailor* (1888). Before examining any possible ethical connections between Melville and Steinbeck, however, their similarities in ethical character are worth mentioning.

---

[7] See Robert DeMott, *Steinbeck's Reading: A Catalogue of Books Owned or Borrowed* (New York: Garland Publishing, 1984) 99. In his essay, "Working at the Impossible: Moby-Dick's Presence in *East of Eden*" (*Steinbeck and the Environment: Interdisciplinary Approaches*, ed. Susan F. Beegel, et al. [Tuscaloosa: University of Alabama Press, 1997] 211–28), DeMott convincingly details the influence of Melville upon Steinbeck's composition. See also DeMott's chapter comparing the artistry of *Moby Dick* and *East of Eden* in *Steinbeck's Typewriter: Essays on his Art* (Troy NY: Whitston Publishing Company, 1996) 74–106.

It is important to note that both Melville and Steinbeck were nonbelievers in any orthodox, Christian sense of the word, yet both found things to value in Christianity or religion generally. At a personal level, Melville was an atheist with little sympathy for religion, but he did find it a useful social tool. In his poem "The House-Top: A Night Piece," from *Battle-Pieces*, Melville describes the draft riots of 1863 as the unleashing of irrational evil and calls the scene "The Atheist roar of riot." Here is the danger: without some framework of ethical and spiritual beliefs, society devolves into chaos. As dyspeptic as Melville may have been about Christianity, he recognized that it was a powerful source for a just ordering of society. At the same time that he rejected Christianity, however, Melville became more reliant than ever upon the Bible for patterns of biblical allusion. These ranged "from a dozen in *Typee* to a 100 in *Mardi* to 250 in *Moby-Dick*...to rise again in *Clarel* to 600 and in *Billy Budd* to 100."[8] Such information, however, speaks only to the author's literary technique and not at all to personal belief.

Although openly disdainful of Christianity as a young man, as he was of nearly any systematic institution, Steinbeck was far more sympathetic toward the beliefs of others than was Melville. One might call it the fascination of a novelist's eye, a ceaseless interest with a mythic structure that stories a people's lives. Despite occasional forays into a church, usually at Elaine Steinbeck's behest, Steinbeck himself was emphatic in his declaration of unbelief. In a letter to Dr. Denton Cox, dated March 5, 1964, Steinbeck explicitly states, "Now finally, I am not religious so that I have no apprehension of a hereafter, either a hope of reward or a fear of punishment" (*LL*, 857). While he did not own religious belief personally, throughout

---

[8] Nathalia Wright, *Melville's Use of the Bible* (Durham: Duke University Press, 1949) 9.

his career Steinbeck remained sympathetic to the beliefs of others, and from approximately 1950 expressed a decidedly moral intent in his work.

While neither Melville nor Steinbeck professed any adherence to Christian beliefs, both of them, however, were well versed in the Bible, particularly the King James Version. Melville's familiarity with Scripture is affirmed by the fact that his extant library contains two personal Bibles, a family Bible and a New Testament and Psalms edition, all heavily penciled in Melville's hand. Steinbeck's personal library held the James Moffat translation of the Bible (1924), *The Living Bible*, a paraphrase translation (1938), and the popular J. B. Phillips translation, *The New Testament in Modern English* (1958). For both authors, the Bible represented a literary treasure-trove of allusions. Sometimes these form a typological pattern sustained throughout a work; at other times they evince a Christian coloring, an almost mythic bed of knowledge in a literary audience of the time. Of Steinbeck's technique, John Antico argues that Steinbeck did not pursue strict biblical parallels, but that "he merely *suggests* religion and Biblical overtones, he actually seems to blur the edges of his analogies so that one feels a religious atmosphere but not a strict and limited Christian reference."[9] In *Steinbeck's Reading* (13–14) Robert DeMott points out that "From his childhood onward, JS was exposed to the Bible (first the King James Version, which he always preferred, then the American Revised Standard Version)." DeMott adds, "Though he was not orthodoxly religious, JS responded powerfully, with an artist's temperament, to the Bible's spirituality, poetical rhythms, symbolism, characterizations and moral dimensions."[10]

[9] John Antico, "A Reading of Steinbeck's 'Flight.'" *Modern Fiction Studies* 11.1 (Spring 1965): 51–52.

[10] DeMott, *Steinbeck's Reading*, 134.

Justice and Just Acts

In *Billy Budd, Sailor,* Melville treks a path as convoluted and dangerous as that left by the monstrous capriciousness of his great white whale. As in *Moby-Dick,* the path Melville ultimately pursues in *Billy Budd* winds through the obscure operations of the human spirit. The quest to decipher humanity's moral consciousness is always elusive, its obliquities always confounding, its goal a wraith impossible to hold or peg down into neatly categorical forms, its very ambiguity the thing that compels Melville irresistibly in its wake.

As modern critics have pursued this direction on the heels of the author, they have seldom concurred on the precise nature of the thing Melville was after in his novella. Edward H. Rosenberry struck to the heart of the matter with his observation that "*Billy Budd* was never conceived as a puzzle for our solution or a choice for our decision, but rather as a course of events for our contemplation."[11] If one were to extrapolate a consensus of critical opinion concerning *Billy Budd,* however, it would come to rest on the nature of justice.

The issue surely forms the theme of the primary narrative—that is, the actual sequence of events transpiring aboard the *Bellipotent*—particularly if one considers justice from a Platonic scheme, as many critics have done. In Plato's thought, justice reveals itself in a tripartite fashion in which justice is at once an internal harmonizing of the individual nature, an order or harmony derived through the state, and an understanding of divine justice or the spiritual ordering of good and evil. The individual, the state, and the divine order, as Plato argues in chapters 13 and 14 of *The Republic,* work in consort to produce

---

[11] Edward H. Rosenberry, "The Problems of *Billy Budd,*" *PMLA* 80 (December 1965): 497.

Justice, an absolute harmony of all life. The elements of the Platonic schematic are readily apparent in *Billy Budd*.[12]

The novella, however, cannot be limited to the topic of justice alone, for such an exclusionary view generally ignores the internal dynamics of innocence and evil. In this latter respect, *Billy Budd* is the capstone of Melville's own ethical pursuit. Here the issue is not simply the conflict of good and evil, but the question of the nature of good and evil themselves. The issue, furthermore, is not simply defining a just act, but exploring the nature of justice itself. William Braswell presents the case thus: "Here Melville is concerned not with the question of why evil exists, but of how man should accept its intricate and desolating effect."[13] These are the questions that Steinbeck also raises in his pursuit of ethical understanding.

In the Billy Budd/Claggart conflict, Melville created one of the most powerful clashes between innocence and evil in American literature. One hesitates to use the term "good" in relation to Budd, for he is not such. Rather, he is naïve, unsullied by the experience of evil. It is here that we see the first resonance with Steinbeck's characters. The victims in his stories are similarly naïve: for example, in *Of Mice and Men* both Curley's wife and Lenny are naïve; when their paths cross they seem destined for mutual destruction. The innocence of Billy Budd, however, is manifested in two ways. First, Melville carefully aligns him with the tradition of the tragic hero—noble, but marred with a fatal flaw. Billy's primary flaw is his

---

[12] See, for example, A. Carl Bredahl, who in *Melville's Angles of Vision* argues that the novella is about justice and focuses his argument on Captain Vere. Rosenberry also argues the theme of justice as the internal ordering of the individual, but sees in it a parallel to Plato's second manifestation of justice as national order.

[13] William Braswell, *Melville's Religious Thought: An Essay in Interpretation* (Durham: Duke University Press, 1943) 122.

speech impediment; his secondary flaws are his volcanic temper and the physical strength to unleash it. The blow that takes Claggart's life is not the first time Billy has vented his anger with his fists. Second, Billy does bear innocence, an intrinsic naiveté that fails to comprehend the designs of evil or the ramifications of reacting to them. Such qualities also come to bear upon many of Steinbeck's characters, and he uses these qualities to highlight the predatory and oppressive forces that oppose the characters.

Melville carefully constructs and sustains the qualities of naïveté, nobility, and innocence of "Baby Budd" in the novella. The "welkin-eyed," twenty-one-year-old Budd "in aspect looked even younger than he was, owing to a lingering adolescent expression in the as yet smooth face, all but feminine in purity of natural complexion."[14] The outer expression is but a manifestation of the inner being. Calling Billy a "child-man," the narrator observes, "a child's utter innocence is but its blank ignorance, and the innocence more or less wanes as intelligence wakes. But in Billy Budd intelligence...had advanced, while yet his simple mindedness remained for the most part unaffected" (78). Billy is the primitive, what Melville deems an "upright barbarian," a clean if not altogether blank slate. As such, Melville describes him as something like Adam "ere the urbane serpent wriggled himself into his company" (17).

If Billy is identifiable with a flawed innocence, Claggart seems readily identifiable with that evil that threatens and destroys innocence. Melville stipulates that his character bears

---

[14] Herman Melville, *Billy Budd, Sailor,* ed. Milton R. Stern (Indianapolis: Bobbs-Merrill, 1975) 14. While there are several fine texts of *Billy Budd* available, this critical edition by Stern, with its full complement of notes and textual detail, is one of the more useful. Further references are cited parenthetically.

a "disdain for innocence" (65). But is he evil, and, if so, how is that evil constituted? In the face of such questions, and as preface for his own excursis into evil as manifested in Claggart, Melville gives his own *apologia*: "But for the adequate comprehending of Claggart by a normal nature, these hints are insufficient. To pass from a normal nature to him one must cross 'the deadly space between.' And this is best done by indirection" (58). That is, we need analogies, or touchstones. Discarding the biblical story of the Fall (59) or Calvin's theology (60), Melville turns to Plato: "In a list of definitions included in the authentic translation of Plato…occurs this: 'Natural Depravity: a depravity according to nature'" (59–60). Melville goes on to describe the characteristics of such a person—sagacious, wily, duplicitous, but most dangerously a secretive nature that qualifies such as madman. In summary, "Something such a one was Claggart, in whom was the mania of an evil nature, not engendered by vicious training or corrupting books or licentious living, but born with him and innate, in short 'a depravity according to nature'" (61).

So too, it seems, evil operates in Steinbeck's characters, at least until the latter stage where he attempts to give *reasons for* actions that are evil because of consequences upon others. Such characters as Cathy Ames for example, are intrinsically flawed. In them, a moral code is fractured in such a way that a monstrous darkness clouds their entire nature. In *East of Eden* Samuel Hamilton reflects, "Names are a great mystery. I've never known whether the name is molded by the child or the child changed to fit the name" (263).[15] In a novel that places so

[15] Hamilton's comments echo chapter 8 from *The Log from the Sea of Cortez*, where Steinbeck reflects, "This name-giving faculty is very highly developed and deeply rooted in our atavistic magics. To name a thing has always been to make it familiar and therefore a little less dangerous to us" (56). Cathy Ames's renaming of herself demonstrates her refusal to be

much emphasis on naming as knowing, nowhere is this ambiguity of evil more evident than in the chameleonic name change of Cathy. She is unknowable. The reader first meets her in chapter 8 as Cathy Ames; by the next chapter it has already slid to Catherine Amesbury (with the play on "buried Ames"). As her names continue to flicker, like an old movie lantern on a cracked screen, from Cathy Trask to Kate Albey, the only thing that centers her character is an ever-increasing diabolicalism. Evil overlaps and consumes whatever face she chooses to wear.

If Steinbeck finds evil innate and intrinsic to one's nature, moreover, he also locates it as a deep and systemic virulence in society. In fact, his later ethics shaded more in this direction. Nonetheless, it is prevalent already in the great works of the 1930s. When a civilization exists to meet its own ends, or in utilitarian terms a selfish happiness at the expense of others, then at such a moment it stands ethically culpable. Taken in sum, then, Steinbeck sees ethical wrong manifested in two ways: the proud individual intent on serving only his or her ends for self-satisfaction or the soulless society intent upon its own self gain at the expense of others' needs. The common factor is a heart blinded by arrogance to and non-interest in others.

Here the nature of evil brings us close to the consonance between Steinbeck and Melville. Rather than seeing evil acts in biblical terms, or in terms of the Fall as elucidated in the western tradition from Augustine to Calvin, evil acts, wrong acts, derive from some fundamental errancy in the individual or in the corporate body. This flaw sets that individual over against the commonwealth of others, and thereby both isolates him and damages others. Thereby justice itself is either threatened or broken. There are indeed ethical problems with

---

domesticated according to social roles; instead, she maintains her own dangerous persona.

this view. For example, if the evil act arises from a malignancy in the individual, one that imbues his entire nature, can that individual be said to have freedom of will? For Melville and Steinbeck, the answer seems to be yes, but that person will choose the wrong thing rather than the good. Why? Because, also in the view of each, that malignancy is pride, the supererogation of the individual will over free will of members of the social context. Melville has alerted us to the fact that his definition of moral evil derives from Plato, and for a full understanding of the ethics at play here, Plato's view merits consideration.

If Plato set the foundations for good and evil in *Phaedo,* the effects of good and evil in the individual and society are elucidated in *The Republic.* Here Plato's aim is pragmatic: to define what justice means and how it can be realized in human society. He works to describe justice as a functioning framework rather than an abstract idea. Plato methodically engages varying views of the state, the necessity of the Guardians, and then arrives at his famous four virtues of the state. *Wisdom* is the knowledge of Rulers as to what is good for the whole community. *Courage* is the Guardians' knowledge of what is or is not to be feared. *Temperance,* also described as harmony, is the understanding of all classes as to who should rule and who obey. *Justice* is the proper use of all three by keeping them distinct. As Plato indicates in chapter 14, moreover, justice appears not only as an external behavior toward others, but also as an internal order of the soul. Injustice is evidence of a damaged soul and internal discord. These ethical qualities are precisely the ones Steinbeck claims in his later work, particularly in reference to *Le Morte* where he saw ideal ethical qualities incarnated in the state.

If Plato's "Myth of Er" (chapter 40) details the rewards of justice after death, the essential preliminary appears in chapter

25, "The Allegory of the Cave." Here Plato unfolds his parable of the soul being imprisoned in the body for past misdeeds and the dangers of plunging untrained minds—these unenlightened souls—into moral discourse. The cave is a world of echoes and shadows, a place, as Plato notes, of "meaningless illusion."[16] When finally exposed to sunlight, and delivered from the land of shadows, the prisoner is blinded. Even worse, however, is when he returns to the nether regions of the cave. Others "would laugh at him and say that he had gone up only to come back with his sight ruined; it was worth no one's while even to attempt the ascent" (231). Indeed, eventually they would have to kill him.

The full implication for our purposes appears in Plato's conclusion to the allegory:

> Wisdom, it seems, is certainly the virtue of some diviner faculty, which never loses its power, though its use for good or harm depends on the direction towards which it is turned. You must have noticed in dishonest men with a reputation for sagacity the shrewd glance of a narrow intelligence piercing the objects to which it is directed. There is nothing wrong with their power of vision, but it has been forced into the service of evil, so that the keener its sight, the more harm it works. (233)

The more evil one's deeds, measured in degrees of harm to others, the less human that person becomes.

The solution to this imbroglio that is unenlightened human nature lies in an order of rule according to Plato's virtues. The philosopher kings have, through innate gifts and long study (ten years study of mathematics), acquired the ability to understand the Ideal Forms. Their task, then, is to translate these into an orderly state to preserve and protect the common

---

[16] Plato, *The Republic*, ed. and trans. Francis MacDonald Cornford (New York: Oxford University Press, 1964) 229. Further quotations will be cited parenthetically.

people not so gifted—those who dwell in the cave. This we call the commonweal. At one point, Steinbeck champions something of an existential ethics, emphasizing personal freedom. In his later work he longed for the Arthurian king, emblematic of supernal justice, the ideal form, who would translate that good for those who dwell in darkness.

Having examined these fundamental ethical structures of good and evil, what conclusions can one make? First, the source of evil seems not to inhere in any particular religious doctrine such as the fall of humanity. While we will see that Steinbeck, as did Melville, uses this doctrine metaphorically, particularly in *East of Eden*, it is not with concurrence with the actual biblical account. However, both Melville and Steinbeck do refer to a world that is irremediably flawed. They vary from the biblical account more on specifics than the general. Second, the source of evil appears to locate in some intrinsic flaw within the nature of humanity itself. Third, that flaw manifests itself in actions that harm the social welfare. As such, in Steinbeck's work at least, we may call such an action a sin against both oneself and humanity. That is to say, wrong actions both diminish what one ideally ought to be—a member of social community—and the community to which the individual ideally belongs. But what kind of action, what intrinsic flaw, accounts for this diminution?

The Self and Sin

For Steinbeck, and this remains consistent throughout the varying stages of his ethical theory, the root sin is arrogance. It may also be called pride, for both terms denote the act of setting oneself—whether the individual or a corporate entity—over against others. Pride diminishes others; it violates the ethical norm we have thus far developed for the commonwealth of all humanity. In *The Seven Deadly Sins*,

Solomon Schimmel writes, "Pride or arrogance—exaggerating our worth and powers, and feeling superior to others—has been recognized since ancient times as a root cause of cruelty and evil."[17]

To summarize Steinbeck's ethics at this point, we would say that the source of evil lies in some fundamental flaw in humans. No one is immune from sin. We all bear the capacity for wrongdoing in our nature and exercise it through wrong choices. Only pride fully satisfies the definition of an ethical vice by the fact that the individual sets himself over (arrogance) and against (separation) society. While the ethical wrong of pride remains a constant in Steinbeck's thinking, the fictional and personal circumstances by which he portrayed this, and the counterpart of an ethical virtue, fluctuated throughout his career. To provide a baseline for this claim, the next chapter investigates his largely failed theory of non-teleological thinking as a basis for ethical actions. The views developed early in his career were informed largely by his fascination with marine biology, but they did influence his sense of right and wrong behavior as expressed in the fiction.

---

[17] Solomon Schimmel, *The Seven Deadly Sins* (New York: Macmillan, 1992).

2

The Early Ethics

A reader finds much to admire, even to praise, in *The Log from the Sea of Cortez*. It ranks among the best of Steinbeck's travel or journalism literature. Its evocative scenery, sense of character, pure eloquence, and frequent playfulness of language rank it alongside *Travels with Charley*. Steinbeck successfully stories a prose argument. Furthermore, it bears the same detail, sense of urgency, and grasp of implications as such works as *The Russian Journal, America and Americans,* and *Letters to Alicia*. In *The Log* we find the journalist's eye for detail and creative statement of it: "All the time we were indulging in courtliness there had been light gunfire on the cliffs, where several men were shooting at black cormorants; and it developed that everyone in Cape San Lucas hates cormorants. They are the flies in a perfect ecological ointment" (58–59). Stories of life on the *Western Flyer* bring a richness and fullness to the work, so that it is from the start half research and half reflection on humans doing the research. The descriptive detail, such as chasing chickens on the beach—"Their legs were like those of ballet dancers and there was no softness in their breasts" (121)—brings the skills of the novelist to the work.

But *The Log* is also, at times, a very confusing work. Clearly, Steinbeck is not aiming to set forth a systematic ethical treatise; nonetheless, his use of ethical terms frequently appears fuzzy and obscure. After claiming that "There is a strong duality in the human which makes for an ethical paradox" (97), he then sets forth the dualistic qualities constituting that paradox. "Of the good," he asserts, "we think always of wisdom, tolerance, kindliness, generosity, humility..." (98). That may be so, but why are these qualities considered good? In what contexts are they so? And, for that matter, what exactly constitutes The Good? Where does the notion come from? Certainly not from the Darwinian, non-teleological thinking he espouses in the book. The qualities are essentially meaningless without some sense of telos, whether it be some Platonic order such as Justice, or some utilitarian ethic, or some sense of obligations.

Similarly unsupported or undeveloped are many of his notions of non-teleological thinking. In a passage that incorporates parts of his "Group-Man" theories,[1] Steinbeck asserts, "Non-teleological notion: that the people we call leaders are simply those who, at the given moment, are moving in the direction behind which will be found the greatest weight, and which represents a future mass movement" (142). The confusion begins with the last clause, which is itself tautological. We don't know if there will be a "future mass movement" and certainly not if the present leader will be a part of it. To speculate so is to do so teleologically. Furthermore, unspoken here is what constitutes that "greatest weight." Is it

---

[1] The sense that biological forces shape the mind and behavior of people in a group, other than the way they would an individual, is the heart of Steinbeck's Group-Man theory. Their view is articulated as early as a June 21, 1933 letter to his friend Carlton Sheffield (see LL 75-77). Steinbeck used the terms the *Phalanx* and the *Mob* with roughly the same equivalence.

an idea, a single person, or a group of persons? Finally, we have to question the use of "direction"; that is, how or by whom is the direction determined? Such issues will provide considerable challenge to the reconstructing of a clear and coherent theory from *The Log*.

That it is necessary to do so in a study of Steinbeck's ethical thinking is beyond question, because non-teleological thinking governed most of his writing throughout the 1930s and had been much on his mind and in his journals and influencing his fiction. *The Sea of Cortez,* first published in 1941 and republished in 1951, with the introductory essay "About Ed Ricketts," is simply a summary statement of that thought. As James C. Kelley has pointed out, "The mix of ecological and mythological concepts pervades much of Steinbeck's work from at least *Tortilla Flat* (1935) to *The Log from the Sea of Cortez* (1951)."[2] However broad the influence of his non-teleological thinking, however, its beginnings antedate the writing of *Tortilla Flat* (summer 1934) by several years (Steinbeck first met Ricketts in a dentist's office in 1930) with his earlier reflections on the Group-Man theory.

The convergence of the lives of Ed Ricketts and John Steinbeck, in both a philosophical mind and also shared interests, almost seems pre-ordained. In his brief but definitive essay, "Philosophy on Cannery Row," Joel W. Hedgpeth traces the convergence of both. At nearly the same time that Ricketts was studying zoology at the University of Chicago, Steinbeck was exploring his interest in marine biology. In summer 1923

---

[2] James C. Kelly, "John Steinbeck and Ed Ricketts: Understanding Life in the Great Tide Pool," *Steinbeck and the Environment: Interdisciplinary Approaches*, ed. Susan F. Beegel, et al. (Tuscaloosa: University of Alabama Press, 1997) 29. See also Richard Astro, *John Steinbeck and Edward F. Ricketts: The Shaping of a Novelist* (Minneapolis: University of Minnesota Press, 1973).

Steinbeck attended a course in zoology at Hopkins Marine Station. In their studies both Ricketts and Steinbeck were apprised of the thinking of William Emerson Ritter, a luminary at the University of California.[3] At the heart of Ritter's teaching and his major publications is the concept of the group formation of organisms, the way in which individual cells or species form larger groups for the benefit of all. Furthermore, Ritter suggested that patterns of such marine organisms are similar to patterns of human organisms. Steinbeck's contribution was to theorize on their latter connection, speculating upon the causes and effects of such parallel organisms.

The Group-Man Theory

The two men shared other common resources, of course, but it does seem that the germ of Group-Man thinking resides in Ricketts and Ritter.[4] From the biological data, however, Steinbeck crafted his own distinct theory. One of the premises of Steinbeck's theory, also mentioned in *The Log* (xliv), is that designed groups, or those integrated by class or social structures, tend to break down. Instead, there must be a more primitive impulse, such as survival, that integrates and moves the group forward. The details of the theory itself begin to emerge more fully in Steinbeck's June 21, 1933, letter to Carlton ("Dook" or "Duke") Sheffield. In this sprawl of ideas and commentary, Steinbeck laid some significant foundational material. In his letter Steinbeck speculates from notes he had been gathering for three years, here linked, as in *The Sea of*

---

[3] See Hedgpeth, "Philosophy on Cannery Row," *Steinbeck: The Man and His Work*, ed. Richard Astro and Tetsumaro Hayashi (Corvallis: Oregon State University Press, 1971) 91–95.

[4] Another such source, according to Hedgpeth, likely included W. C. Allee, *Animal Aggregations* (Chicago: University of Chicago Press, 1931).

Cortez, to marine biology. He observes that the work of the coral building an atoll is not unlike human groups that have worked to build, for example, a Gothic spire. No one coral can build an atoll; no one person can build a Gothic spire. Steinbeck concludes, "When acting as a group, men do not partake of their ordinary natures at all." Some unique force empowers the group so that it becomes a new living organism that subsumes its "individual parts" (*LL,* p. 76). In a letter written a few days later to George Albee, Steinbeck reiterates the theme, here introducing the term "phalanx" to describe this group action. Again, the premise is biological:

> A further arrangement of cells and a very complex one may make a unit which we call a man. That has been our final unit. But there have been mysterious things which could not be explained if man is the final unit. He also arranges himself into larger units, which I have called the phalanx. The phalanx has its own memory—memory of the great tides when the moon was close, memory of starvations when the food of the world was exhausted...and the phalanx has emotions of which the unit man is incapable.....You have heard about the trickiness of the MOB. Mob is simply a phalanx, but if you try to judge a mob nature by the nature of its men units, you will fail as surely as if you tried to understand a man by studying one of his cells. (*LL,* 79–80)

The idea of an evolutionary memory is echoed in *The Log* (31–34), but this letter also contains the germ of *In Dubious Battle* as Steinbeck describes "the trickiness of the MOB," and, in fact, he concludes the letter by announcing his intention to write a novel with this as its theme. Ed Ricketts, he adds in the letter to Albee, has "dug up all the scientific material." Thus, the trip recorded in *The Sea of Cortez,* taken during March and April 1940, and *In Dubious Battle,* probably started in late 1933 and published in 1936, share their roots in Steinbeck's work in marine biology and his intimate association with Ricketts.

The jump from *The Sea of Cortez* to the mob, a theory that influenced not only *In Dubious Battle* but also *The Grapes of Wrath* and *Cannery Row,* needs an extra step, however. This Brian Railsback provides in his essay "Searching for 'What Is'": "*The Sea of Cortez* was for John Steinbeck what the Galapagos Archipelago was for Darwin: A pristine panorama of the natural world, perfect for the illustration of profound interpretations of biology."[5] Steinbeck suggests as much when he draws an analogy with Darwin in *The Log*:

> On this day, the sun glowing on the morning beach made us feel good. It reminded us of Charles Darwin, who arrived late at night on the *Beagle* in the Bay of Valparaiso. In the morning he awakened and looked ashore and he felt so well that he wrote, "When morning came everything appeared delightful. After Tierra del Fuego, the climate felt quite delicious, the atmosphere so dry and the heavens so clear and blue with the sun shining brightly, that all nature seemed sparkling with life" (*Voyage of the Beagle,* Chapter 12, July 23). Darwin was not saying how it was with Valparaiso, but rather how it was with him. (195)

One might extend the analogy further and see *The Log* as a companion to Darwin's notebook.

According to Railsback, one of the most influential books on the thinking of Steinbeck and Ricketts was Jan Christian Smuts's *Holism and Evolution*.[6] The significance of Smuts lay not just in his emulation of Darwin as the great synthesizer of biology, but also his belief that if Darwin's theory is a creative view, as Smuts argued, then it is also progressive, a "form of

---

[5] Brian Railsback, "Searching for What Is," *Steinbeck and the Environment*, 127.

[6] Jan Christian Smuts, *Holism and Evolution* (New York: Macmillan, 1926) 218.

comradeship, of social co-operation and mutual help."[7] In such thinking, Steinbeck at least found reinforcement for his Group-Man theory. Both influences appear to be summarized in a comment from Steinbeck in *The Log*:

> There is tied up to the most primitive and powerful racial or collective instinct a rhythm sense of "memory" which affects everything and which in the past was probably more potent than it is now. It would at least be more plausible to attribute these profound effects to devastating and instinct-searing tidal influences active during the formative times of the early race history of organism; and whether or not any mechanism has been discovered or is discoverable to carry on this imprint is there. The imprint is in us.... (33)

The Group Man theory is the focus of *In Dubious Battle,* usually under Doc Burton's careful questioning of the radical leader Mac (Ed Ricketts served as prototype for Burton). Doc reflects, "'A man in a group isn't himself at all, he's a cell in an organism that isn't like him any more than the cells in your body are like you'" (*IDB* 144–145). But Doc, whom Mac describes as too far left to be a Communist, remains skeptical of the Group Man. Why? What is left out? Steinbeck himself had discovered the answer in the process of writing *In Dubious Battle,* and it is the same thing that non-teleological thinking, paradoxically, strives for: tenderness and compassion for other individuals. Doc Burton has these qualities; Mac and later Jim Nolan totally lack them. "We can't think about the hurts of one man. It's necessary, Doc," says Mac at one point. Doc replies, "I wasn't questioning your motives, nor your ends. I was just sorry for the poor old man. His self-respect is down. That's a bitter thing to him, don't you think so, Mac?" To which Mac

[7] Ibid.

replies sharply, "I can't take time to think about the feelings of one man. I'm too busy with big bunches of men" (*IDB* 201).

It is doubtful whether Steinbeck was ever completely satisfied with his Group-Man theory. It was an exciting theory, new and challenging, and its analogy to marine biology certainly attracted him. Moreover, it contained a degree of truth—people in a mob act differently from the way they act as individuals—that provided a powerful theme for *In Dubious Battle* and *The Grapes of Wrath*. Within each of these novels, however, and in all the later works Steinbeck offers an alternative to the Group Man: the compassionate and creative individual. To John O'Hara he wrote in 1949:

> I think I believe one thing powerfully—that the only creative thing our species has is the individual, lonely mind. Two people can create a child but I know of no other thing created by a group. The group ungoverned by individual thinking is a horrible destructive principle. The great change in the last 2,000 years was the Christian idea that the individual soul was very precious. Unless we can preserve and foster the principle of preciousness of the individual mind, the world of men will either disintegrate into a screaming chaos or will go into a grey slavery. And that fostering and preservation seem to me our greatest job. (*LL* 359–60)

In his memoir of Ed Ricketts in *The Log from the Sea of Cortez*, Steinbeck reflects on the Group-Man theory and finds it wanting: "The creative principle is a lonely and an individual matter. Groups can correlate, investigate, and build, but we could not think of any group that has ever created or invented anything. Indeed, the first impulse of the group seems to be to destroy the creation and the creator" (xiv). In fact, at the end of *The Sea of Cortez* Steinbeck covers his philosophical bets with a disclaimer: "The safety-valve of all speculation is: *It might be so*" (265).

Non-teleological Thinking

While the Group-Man theory appears haphazardly, but seems to have had substantial influence upon his fiction, the premises of non-teleological thinking as set forth in *The Log* do seem more orderly, if not always logically structured. Two reasons account for this. The first is the strategy of the travel narrative. This has purpose, direction, and, to use a thoroughly teleological term, a goal. It was, as Steinbeck himself thought, an adventure, and that constitutes the second unifying structure. The reader meets characters and events that startle and delight. Steinbeck's great talent for illuminating minor characters, who otherwise might be forgettable in the whole, is nowhere more in evidence than here. Upon these two structures Steinbeck pegs bits and pieces of his theory.

Both teleological and non-teleological thinking arise from a human perspective on reality. They assume a trait of humanity to so construct a perspective; that is, reason. In spite of all the difficulties such an assumption makes for Steinbeck's theory, he rather adroitly sidesteps it altogether and dives directly into the easier waters of speculation. If while doing so he might pose some philosophical cautions, it comports perfectly with the reflective and speculative attitude of the adventure. Thereby he first provides this on teleological thinking:

> What we personally conceive by the term "teleological thinking," as exemplified by the notion about the shiftless unemployed, is most frequently associated with the evaluating of causes and effects, the purposiveness of events. This kind of thinking considers changes and cures—what "should be" in the terms of an end pattern (which is often a subjective or an anthropomorphic projection); it presumes the bettering of conditions, often, unfortunately, without achieving more than a most superficial understanding of those conditions. (138)

The faults of such thinking, of striving for a specific goal or *telos*, are several. First, such a thinker tends to avoid facts or realities that don't fit into his predetermined *telos*. Second, if such variances arise the teleological thinker tends to bend facts to theory. Finally, such a thinker is tempted to manipulate conditions or observations to fit the way "things should be" according to his theory.

Non-teleological thinking tries everywhere and at all times to be objective as to the data. Thus, Steinbeck defines it: "Non-teleological thinking concerns itself primarily not with what should be, or could be, or might be, but rather with what actually 'is'—attempting at most to answer the already sufficiently difficult questions *what* or *how*, instead of *why*" (139). This he calls "is" thinking, seeing deeply and clearly what exists in fact rather than in theory. It is the very definition of realism: to collect the data, to show an accurate portrait, to tell the truth about an event.

Almost as a side note, Steinbeck slips into his discussion of definitions a comment on the effect of non-teleological thinking on human behavior and relationships. Here is the problem. With this intense focus upon objective reality, non-teleologists might be thought to be hard, remote, even cruel. As Steinbeck observes, "Quite the opposite seems to be true. Non-teleological methods more than any other seem capable of great tenderness, of an all-embracingness which is rare otherwise" (149). Such a comment is of course an ethical claim. It is also a virtue that appears often in his early works.

With his distinction between the two kinds of thinking made, Steinbeck relates it once again to the Group Man. Dispensing with "what we have in mind," with "cause in thinking and blame in feeling," and with any mystical symbols, Steinbeck asserts that

> The truest reason for anything's being so is that it *is*. This is actually and truly a reason, more valid and clearer than all the other separate reasons, or than any group of them short of the whole. Anything less than the whole forms part of the picture only, and the infinite whole is unknowable except by *being* in it, by living into it. (151–152)

With this sense of "living into" and "being in it," Steinbeck extrapolates from biology to humanity.

His premise is that all groups are relational:

> Our own interest lay in relationships of animal to animal. If one observes in this relational sense, it seems apparent that species are only commas in a sentence, that each species is at once the point and the base of a pyramid, that all life is relational to the point where an Einsteinian relativity seems to emerge. And then not only the meaning but the feeling about species grows misty. One merges into another, groups melt into ecological groups until the time when what we know as life meets and enters what we think of as non-life: barnacle and rock, rock and earth, earth and tree, tree and rain and air. And the units nestle into the whole and are inseparable from it. (218)

Earlier we examined how this might be so in the tide pool: protection, survival, and reproduction. In a strictly Darwinian and biological sense, and that is the only one Steinbeck operates under here, the same may be said for humanity. But he pushes the paradigm further to a strictly naturalist accounting:

> And it is a strange thing that most of the feeling we call religious, most of the mystical outcrying which is one of the most prized and used and desired reactions of our species, is really the understanding, and the attempt to say that man is

> related to the whole thing, related inextricably to all reality, known and unknowable. (218)[8]

The summary, wrote Steinbeck, is that "all things are one thing and that one thing is all things" (218).

Ethical Variances

The immediate question is whether Steinbeck, in his speculations ranging from tide pool to human nature, ever broaches anything like an ethical construct. Everything in his nature-centered world appears to mitigate against it. He has stripped any divine imprimatur for right action from his world, and repeatedly denigrates what he calls a "mystical" response to this world. On at least three specific occasions, however, he addresses the issue: Given this, how then should one act?

The first of these tendentiously addresses the problem of evil. Steinbeck has argued that hope is a quality of humanity; it is observable even if one can't account for its origins. In a rather long and wandering excursis, Steinbeck sets forth his premise:

> It is amazing how the strictures of the old teleologies infect our observation, causal thinking warped by hope. It was said earlier that hope is a diagnostic human trait, and this simple cortex symptom seems to be a prime factor in our inspection of our universe. For hope implies a change from a present bad condition to a future better one. The slave hopes for freedom, the weary man for rest, the hungry for food. And the feeders of hope, economic and religious, have from these simple strivings of dissatisfaction managed to create a world picture which is very hard to escape. Man grows toward perfection; animals grow toward man; bad grows toward good; and down toward

[8] As exemplars of this thought Steinbeck includes Jesus, St. Augustine, St. Francis, Roger Bacon, and Charles Darwin, none of whom, including Darwin, would go to that extreme.

> up, until our little mechanism, hope, achieved in ourselves probably to cushion the shock of thought, manages to warp our whole world. (88–89)

We must be careful here, for Steinbeck clearly attributes hope to teleological thinkers, those who refuse to live in the moment. He does go on to say that man "is the only animal who lives outside of himself, whose drive is in external things" (90). Despite the derisive comments that follow about such men, two important questions arise. First, if hope is a singular trait of humanity, buried deep in the cortex, then this must be "man as is." To find contemptible the ways that hope is exercised may surely be legitimate thinking, but it is not "is-thinking." Steinbeck may find the poisonous boteta fish nearly beautiful because of its place in the whole, yet he condemns humanity for exercising a natural, inborn trait of its very nature. Second, if hope is a thing to be derided, then how does humanity account for any self-transcending achievement? In a caricature of hope, Steinbeck wrote:

> For in spite of overwhelming evidence to the contrary, the trait of hope still controls the future, and man, not a species, but a triumphant race, will approach perfection, and, finally, tearing himself free, will march up the stars and finally take his place where, because of his power and virtue, he belongs. (91)

Apart from the parodic qualities of the above, Steinbeck firmly entrenches himself outside the community of hope, those whose lives become obsessed by chasing some dream. Throughout this period, though, he also wrote brilliantly of characters longing for just such a dream. One may ask, finally, what we have in lieu of hope. Not hopelessness, to be sure. That would be a self-defeating tautology based on the premise that there is such a thing as hope to lose. Instead, we have the Group—surviving, protecting, reproducing. And nothing more.

A second general issue of ethics that enters *The Log* is duties. If, as was discussed in the first chapter, ethical choices take place and affect a community, then what is one's duty to that community? Or is it entirely to oneself? Duties or obligations lie at the heart of nearly any ethical theory, because they focus upon right or wrong conduct in community. It might be said that the swarms of living creatures Steinbeck observed exercise co-operation. For their well-being (survival, reproduction, and protection) they swarm together. The group, if not guarantees, at least assures a degree of ongoing life of the species. If we could say, as Steinbeck appears to do so, that, grounded on the same three-fold needs, life is the highest good of the species, then the subject of ethics would be greatly simplified. Our duties are those that further the life of the species.

This does appear to be Steinbeck's stance, for he relegates the whole subject of duties to the teleologists, and duties, therefore, of little account.

> The lies we tell about our duty and our purposes, the meaningless words of science and philosophy, are walls that topple before a bewildered little "why." Finally, we learned to know why we did these things. The animals were very beautiful. Here was life from which we borrowed life and excitement. In other words, we did these things because it was pleasant to do them. (213)

And if, as he says, one does things "because it was pleasant to do them," then he has abdicated a life of principle for one of hedonism. Steinbeck is certainly correct about this: a life lived according to duties and obligations *is* teleological. Such a life sees ends and purposes that are beneficial to others in the community and one lives in accord with those ends. Obligation requires one to act against one's self-interest at times in order to contribute to the well-being of community and the definition of the personal character of others.

In his abhorrence of the social decree "It should be so," and with his steadfast search for beauty in things as they are, it is no surprise that Steinbeck wrote little of duties and obligations. In fact, his well-known concluding summary to *The Log* intensifies his present-oriented belief: "The safety-valve of all speculation is: *It might be so*. And as long as that *might* remains, a variable deeply understood, then speculation does not easily become dogma, but remains the fluid creative thing it might be" (266). Such an ethic, he believed, held freedom for individual speculation and action. This is not a strictly utilitarian view in the mode of Jeremy Bentham and John Stuart Mill. Rather, it resonates with the pre-utilitarian view of hedonism, in which pleasure itself is the highest principle. It is necessary to highlight these traits because they contrast with his later ethical views, where Steinbeck did in fact develop a deontological ethic mindful of the duties and obligations of humans in community.

A third significant trait of Steinbeck's ethical views here in the early years is the principle of discrimination. The Group-Man theory does serve as a coherent evolutionary theory for the development of humanity. Often Steinbeck speaks of a "primordial memory," that stirring and directive sense for survival evident in sea creatures also. In *The Log* he states it like this: "For the ocean, deep and black in the depths, is like the low dark levels of our minds in which the old dream symbols incubate and sometimes rise up to sight" (31). For him, the sea is not simply an analogy, but a birthing of humanity, the vestiges of which remain in us. These include, among others, the coalescence into groups for reproduction, for protection, for survival. As humanity evolved, these traits developed into basic human necessities. As Steinbeck put it in *The Log*, a human is "one factor in a surge of striving" (167). The biological basis of the Group-Man theory follows soundly from such observations.

But paradoxes and contradictions exist within Steinbeck's theory also. It may well do for self-indulgent reflection under a warm Mexican sun. In *The Log*, Steinbeck himself praises "laziness" as the necessary state of contemplation. Possibly so, but Steinbeck, who philosophizes while eschewing the title of philosopher does stretch the boundaries of logic and consistency in the Group-Man theory. Foremost among these is the much-diminished role of the individual. Steinbeck appears to recognize this:

> In pure creativeness, in art, in music, in mathematics, there are no true collaborations. The creative principle is a lonely and an individual matter. Groups can correlate, investigate, and build, but we could not think of any group that has ever created or invented anything. Indeed, the first impulse of the group seems to be to destroy the creation and the creator. But integration, or the designed group, seems to be highly vulnerable. (xliv)

Furthermore, the fiction of the 1930s emphasizes the loneliness of the individual in conflict *with* group forces. We have to ask, then, whether there are means by which an individual transcends the group. In biology we call it "aberration." In humanity we call it "individualism." Is there the prospect of the autonomous human?

A second major issue of the Group-Man theory finds its roots in Aristotle's masterpiece of biological investigation, *De Partibus Animalium*.[9] Aristotle's genius was for classification;

[9] Robert DeMott includes in *Steinbeck's Reading: A Catalogue of Books Owned and Borrowed* ([New York: Garland, 1984]) these works by Aristotle: *Historia Animalium, De Partibus Animalium,* and *Physica,* and points out Steinbeck's reference in his forward to *Between Pacific Tides:*

nowhere is this more notable than in his biological studies. The essential point about these studies (seen also in the *Historia Animalium*) is that Aristotle did not approach plant and animal biology as wholly other than human, but as an order in which humanity finds its unique place. In this respect, Aristotle's was a new voice both in Greek philosophy (he specifically challenges Empedocles, Anaxagoras, and Democritus) and also in modern biology. Consider in brief his method first, then its effects with their consequences for the Group-man theory. The fittingness of the comparison inheres in the fact that both Aristotle and Steinbeck begin from similar premises.

While Steinbeck often disavows the term *analogy* when reflecting on tide pool to human nature, all the while doing exactly that, Aristotle makes as a fundamental premise that all life shares a unity through what he calls *soul*:

> If now this something that constitutes the form of the living being be the soul, or part of the soul, or something that without the soul cannot exist; as would seem to be the case, seeing at any rate that when the soul departs, what is left is no longer a living animal, and that none of the parts remain what they were before, excepting in mere configuration, like the animals that in the fable are turned to stone; if, I say, this is so, then it will come within the province of the natural philosopher to inform himself concerning the soul, and to treat of it, either in its entirety, or, at any rate, of that part of it which constitutes the essential character of an animal.[10]

"Aristotle built a world and we are building one. His was a true world and ours is. And the two need not meet and quarrel" (v).

[10] Aristotle, *De Partibus Animalium* (639b 16–641b 29). *Aristotle's Selections,* ed. W. D. Ross (New York: Charles Scribner's Sons, 1955) 165. This edition of Aristotle's works will be used throughout for ease of convenience.

Soul, then, is the living essence of an animal, one in which all animate beings participate. Within this general context, species are individuated. According to Aristotle, though, we may speak of analogy in a generalized sense; that is the spine of a fish to the spine of a man. Other similarities or "analogies" exist, for in every instance and every species "The body too must be somehow or other be made for the soul" (177). With so much Steinbeck would likely be in agreement. The major distinction occurs where Aristotle introduces his concept of the ratiocinative soul in *De Anima*.

If Aristotle believes that soul is a property of all living things, and that the four definitive qualities of soul include the nutritive and sensitive; animals may be nutritive, sensitive, and bear movement, but only humans also possess the ratiocinative faculty. Humans can confront options, decide upon the best option, and act upon that decision. It remained for the *Nicomachean Ethics* of course for Aristotle to define what those "best" options were. At this point, and of significance to our study of Steinbeck's ethics at this point, is Aristotle's conclusion that "What comes last and is possessed by fewest is reasoning and thought; for among mortals those that possess reasoning possess also all the others, but those that possess each of these do not all possess reasoning; some do not possess even imagination, and others live by this alone" (207). Humans alone possess this critical fourth property of reason.

It should be evident that Steinbeck's world, as revealed in *The Log*, is a more narrow, more constricted one than Aristotle's. Steinbeck fails to account for humans as individuated species, even while faithfully classifying and cataloging those species he finds in the tide pools. Left unstated is the question: What identifies humanity as a species? An answer is implied in the prose itself. The descriptive imagery implies creative skill and imagination. The reflective passages imply the gift for appreciation of beauty, which Steinbeck does herald at several points. The very act of planning such a venture, of fulfilling it by charting a course and by carefully cataloging specimens implies a rational act. Yet, by force of non-teleological is-thinking, Steinbeck confines himself to the moment.

Steinbeck's Naturalist Ethics

Finally, then, we have to explore in what ethical state Steinbeck stands during the early years of his career. To say that the stance is naturalistic would be accurate, but also incomplete, for naturalism developed as both a literary approach and a philosophical position. Both of these apply to Steinbeck.

As a literary approach, naturalism evolved out of turn-of-the-century realism. To step back for a moment, nineteenth-century literature seemed dominated by twin towers. On one side stood the vestiges of Enlightenment thinking with the supreme god of reason. From this tower emanated a literature of political discussion, of memoir and autobiography, of novels as carefully plotted as a board game and of matters a whole lot less interesting. Life as an Enlightenment thinker was not particularly interesting since they eschewed all things flamboyant or colorful. Especially they dusted these tidy shelves of the imagination and sentiment.

The Romantics, it seemed, found their very delight in the things the Enlightenment rejected. Philip Freneau wrote on "The Wild Honeysuckle" and "On a Honey Bee," subjects unfit for Enlightenment consideration. While Thomas Paine wrote "On Common Sense," one of the best political tracts and worst theological inquiries in our nation's history, William Cullen Bryant wrote "A Forest Hymn," a piece that inspired little and unsettled no one but was *prima facie* evidence for Romantic license. But mostly the Romantics wrote about humanity—humanity with all its untidy foibles, ostensible follies, and enduring pathos. Humans could never be controlled by any sort of Enlightenment creed, doctrine, or philosophy.

Perhaps no literary movement is complete, however, until an official critical analysis of it has been made. Thus it remained for William Dean Howells to define realism in his *Criticism and Fiction*. After condemning those who said that authors should imitate the style and subjects of those authors of the past, Howells encourages them to focus upon life as they find it now. Howells indicts the critics who make the writer of "every-day life" feel insufficient. The writer, moreover, works not to propagate a moral or to further an agenda, but to entertain the "common reader." Thus realism consists of "fidelity to experience and probability of motive."[11] It would be hard to find one word there with which Steinbeck could disagree.

With this focus of literarily "living-in-the-moment," exploring what is and what might be instead of what should be, Howells opened the door between realism and naturalism. Steinbeck stands in the naturalistic side of the door. He stands in the company of such other American writers as Stephen Crane, Bret Harte, Theodore Dreiser, and Upton Sinclair. Steinbeck's home as a naturalist appears stronger yet as we turn from literary naturalism to philosophical naturalism. The former is a method of writing about things of this world—unbiased, objective, and realistic. The latter is a means by which one beholds the world. Here too, in this early stage, we find Steinbeck of the naturalist mind.

Although it is common practice to affiliate naturalism with a twentieth-century world and life view, a sort of birth canal

---

[11] William Dean Howells, *Criticism and Fiction and Other Essays* (New York: Greenwood, 1977).

for modernism, naturalism had been stewing in its primal waters for well over a century prior. Many philosophers date it to Thomas Malthus's *Principles of Population* (1798). Malthus used mathematical formulas to demonstrate that humanity would outstrip its food supplies and would begin a process of self-extermination simply because there is not enough supply to support life. Thus there would be a struggle for survival. Darwin set out on his 1831 tour aboard the *Beagle* for different reasons. Instead of a theoretician, as was Malthus, he was a scientist, collecting the data, examining similarities and differences, and arriving deductively at conclusions. These included the Adaptation of Species, where the survival and characteristics of a species lay in adaptation to the laws of nature, and the Theory of Selection, where adapted species survive and less well-adapted species become extinct. Hence, we have the development of life according to natural law, or, evolution. Such was the biological status of naturalism into the twentieth century, and so too Steinbeck is positioned.

Biological naturalism must be synthesized with the changing world and life views of the Enlightenment, romanticism, and realism alluded to earlier. Each of these also signaled huge shifts in human relationships with the divine that finally defined naturalism. For all sorts of reasons, the Enlightenment disavowed God's presence in immediate human affairs.[12] Instead, they relegated God, under the rubric of Deism, to some vague, amorphous space in the universe, wholly uninvolved in and unconcerned about human affairs. And that was just fine because those humans equipped to rule had reason, which more than sufficed.

---

[12] Among such reasons were political dissension over the divine right of kings, a need for individual freedom, particularly during the French Revolution, and what some saw as onerous rules of religious doctrines.

The romantics believed it did not. In fact, they believed rationalism had scoured the human spirit of the very things that make us human: emotions, pleasure, relationships, and the like. The romantic believed one may have some experience, perhaps sensorily, of the divine. It might be appropriate to speak of an experiential God; that is, one knows God as one experiences God individually, not doctrinally. For the romantic, this life in all its multifaceted experiences, was the end matter of inquiry. Such a view, as we have seen earlier, hardened into diamond-edged belief with the realists. The great difference was that while the romantic often viewed life as a sunny place, even though impeded at times by great yearnings of the heart and dramatic melancholia, the realist found the world a hard and uncompromising place, a home of shadows and wailing spirits.

Naturalism placed the seal of approval upon the most abject psychological turmoil of realism. We have no right to be happy, and the world is going to get us if we try, which leads to a definition of naturalism. On the one hand it is a way of looking at life that seems without any external, supranatural, and ordering guidance. Naturalism is a temperament, a feeling that the presence of disorder in this life is simply too large to cope with. On the other hand, naturalism answers to a philosophical definition. Its presupposition is that there is no God present in the world, but that humanity is subject to the forces of natural law. Instead of a spirit determined by God, humanity is a physical, molecular structure determined by forces beyond its control. C. S. Lewis, who spent his apologetic career inveighing against naturalism, nonetheless gave us one of the best short definitions of it: "By Naturalism we mean the doctrine that only Nature—the whole interlocked system—exists. And if that were true, every thing and event would, if we knew enough, be explicable without remainder...as a necessary product of the system."[13]

The large picture of humanity in Steinbeck's fiction remains a naturalistic one in which people struggle within and against natural forces and are partly victims of them. As such, the philosophy of naturalism constitutes Steinbeck's essential view of humanity. Naturalists assume the right to determine one's own meaning, to assert that knowledge autonomously discovered (rather than revealed by any supranatural source) is authentic and final. This, as Steinbeck called it, is "is-thinking." In *Naturalism* by Goetz and Taliaferro, the authors set the case thus: "Given that strict naturalism maintains that all explanation is nonpurposive in nature and the human self or ego and its activity are part of a deterministic causal nexus, it is not surprising that strict naturalism also claims that there is no radical bifurcation between a person or self and its physical body."[14] In other words, what we are is who we are. This highly evolved complex of chemicals and tissues and bone constitutes the animal we call human.

These views also are in evidence in Steinbeck's early fiction and affect the ethical situations characters find themselves in. For example, in his haunting story "Flight," accidental circumstances are present and direct the tale of Pepe. Pepe's doom is fixed from the earliest lines—in the hot, oppressive coastal environment; in his desire to be a man; but mostly in the subconscious flick of his knife like a serpent's darting tongue. The preponderance of snake imagery in the story is of a piece with the deadly act and the theme. Some ancient darkness shapes and determines the way Pepe will go. In "John

---

[13] C. S. Lewis, *Miracles: A Preliminary Study* (New York: Macmillan, 1947, 1973) 17.

[14] Stewart Goetz and Charles Taliaferro, *Naturalism* (Grand Rapids: Wm. B. Eerdmans, 2008) 17–18.

Steinbeck: Naturalism's Priest," Woodburn O. Ross describes the development of Steinbeck's naturalistic view to the date of the article (1949), but Ross is one of the few to point out that, although Steinbeck's premises are naturalistic, he often violates his own premises: "Steinbeck's naturalistic ideas have clearly done much to determine the character of the fiction which he writes. Yet to describe him as a naturalist is in one sense false. The description is incomplete; for, while never repudiating the points of view which I have just described, he amalgamates them with others which many would consider contradictory."[15]

It may be tempting, finally, that by designating Steinbeck's early ethics as naturalistic, one is thereby, and in self-contradiction, claiming that it is really not an ethical position at all. But that is not the case. In his essay defining ethical naturalism, Nicholas L. Sturgeon states the case thus:

> [The] issue is whether values and obligations, especially moral values and moral obligations, fit into a scientifically based, naturalistic view of the world. Ethical naturalism is understood as the view that they do. It holds, more specifically, (a) that such ethical properties as the goodness of persons, character traits, and other things, and such as the rightness or wrongness of actions, are natural properties of the same general sort as properties investigated by the sciences, and (b) that they are to be investigated in the same general way that we investigate those properties.[16]

More specifically, Sturgeon states the challenge to a naturalistic ethic:

> A naturalistic worldview, however, is virtually always understood to be one that at the very least rejects belief in the

[15] Woodburn O. Ross, "John Steinbeck: Naturalism's Priest," *College English* 10 (May 1949): 433–34.

[16] Nicholas L. Sturgeon, "Ethical Naturalism," *The Oxford Handbook of Ethical Theory*, ed. David Copp (Oxford: Oxford University Press, 2006) 92.

> supernatural, so part of the issue under debate is what place there is for moral values and obligations in a world without a God or gods and without supernatural commands or sanctions. It of course continues to be a hotly debated issue in philosophy whether any such naturalistic metaphysical picture is correct.[17]

If not correct, then any naturalistic ethics arises from two sources. The first has already been named by Steinbeck as characteristics of the tide pool—protection, reproduction, and survival. But there has to be more than this, or else humans are animals. Perhaps the ethical quality that countermands these tide pool traits is decency. Upon this quality human behavior, even within a naturalistic ethic, maybe judged.

Decency, moreover, is more than mere social convention—usually stated as the ethical guide in a naturalistic ethics. True, animals survive by certain conventions typical of their species. So do humans. But decency is an awareness of the intrinsic worth of other humans. Cannibalism, for example, is wrong not only because it is unconventional but also because it is indecent as we have defined it. If this is so, then it seems that decency works two ways. First, it is the way community *holds* an individual. Does it honor that individuality even within the group, or is it the oppressive force that Steinbeck constantly exposes in the fiction of the 1930s? Second, decency is signified by how that individual *acts* in community, either enabling others or denigrating and destroying them. Such would seem to be Steinbeck's stance, naturalistic in philosophical positioning, championing a creed of decency as an ethical guideline to right action.

---

[17] Ibid.

3

The Grapes of Wrath: The Emergence of an Ethics

The ethical issues of *The Grapes of Wrath* are actually the consequence of its three related stories. Each lends considerable depth and understanding to Steinbeck's masterpiece. Consider that claim in the light of alternate critical approaches. Essentially, a literary scholar positions herself in one of two ways when "confronting" a work of literature. One method is to slice off one ring of meaning, almost like an onion. This is called a theme. What the scholar says about it is a thesis. But even when the act of exploring that single ring is done, many more layers remain to discover the whole. Steinbeck once spoke of *The Grapes of Wrath*'s having five layers of meaning. In fact there are many more. Some other works are clad in a layer of meaning so gauzy and thin one can hardly find it. This whole effort, which we may simply call literary analysis, should be understood as an act of projection. Meaning accumulates. The whole grows more solid and weighty.

The other important bookend that props our understanding of the central work is what events and influences preceded it. For various reasons this approach has been controversial in the history of critical affairs, even labeled at one time with that dreaded name "biographical criticism," before which every knee shivered. Just when this strange sense of the inefficacy of biographical study first appeared, or when the funeral bells tolled its passing, is hard to calibrate. Nonetheless, this retrospective critical approach, reviewing some events and writings that attended the composition of a larger whole, is essential to an understanding of Steinbeck's ethical voice in *The Grapes of Wrath*. These are the interior stories that shaped the living essence of the exterior telling.

We have little evidence of Steinbeck's personal involvement with the migrants before 1936. While Steinbeck remained largely unaware of and uninvolved in the political turmoil already stirring California in the early 1930s, his wife Carol Steinbeck had grown into an increasingly radical liberal. Her friend Sis Reamer first pointed Steinbeck toward some engagement with political issues. Reamer was a fundraiser for the Communist efforts to organize labor and was therefore well known by the leaders of the movement. It was she who introduced Steinbeck to one of the leaders, Cecil McKiddy, whose stories later found their way into *In Dubious Battle* and also into the Peach Strike at the Tagus Ranch in *The Grapes of Wrath*.[1] Steinbeck used the material successfully, creating a best-selling and sensational novel in *In Dubious Battle*. But was the subject matter only that, or was it forming a deeper pull upon him?

Steinbeck started that year of 1936 with what he called his "flock of experimentation," clearly a reference to his writing for the stage in *Of Mice and Men*. The work began in earnest in March and was finished in August. Here Steinbeck's perspective changed. Instead of writing about the Mob, or the Group Man, he turned to a dramatic portrait of two isolated

---

[1] In Jackson J. Benson's opinion, "McKiddy seems to have contributed to the composite that would make up the character Tom Joad," and his uncle, a lay preacher, a model for Jim Casy. See "The Background to the Composition of *The Grapes of Wrath*," *Critical Essays on Steinbeck's* The Grapes of Wrath, ed. John Ditsky (Boston: G. K. Hall, 1989) 53.

bindlestiffs, representative of the longing of the migrants everywhere in California. About the time he completed *Of Mice and Men,* George West of the *San Francisco News* approached Steinbeck with the idea of writing a series of articles on the disturbing conditions in the agricultural belt of the San Joaquin Valley. The focus was to be the plight of the migrants and the government's efforts to supply sanitary camps for them.

The idea appealed to Steinbeck immediately. Outfitting an old bakery truck in a manner foreshadowing the 1960 trip in *Rocinante,* he set out for the squatters' camps in the company of the director in charge of management of migrant camp programs, Eric H. Thomsen. This trip imprinted the human misery and need on him as never before. Throughout the 1930s between 300,000 and 400,000 migrants had arrived in California. The shabby camps of broken dreams exuded tragedy. In his journalistic entries, each rendered in terse, clipped, unornamented prose, Steinbeck told their representative stories. This series of articles, later gathered in one collection as *The Harvest Gypsies,* might be deemed the first book of *The Grapes of Wrath.*

Thomsen knew how he wanted to proceed when he guided the novelist. They rode randomly through the Central Valley, meandering from one squalid shantytown to another. Here lived the poorest of the poor—semiliterate, unskilled laborers. Beside the natural threats of flood and drought, hunger and thirst, these migrants had faced every tactic in the landowners' manual to evict them from the land, from vigilante squads to bribes. All the time Thomsen and Steinbeck angled south until at last they arrived at the government-run Arvin "sanitary" camp just south of Bakersfield. Faithfully reconstructed in *The Grapes of Wrath,* these camps were a safe haven, a respite center to regather one's strength. This first trip (Steinbeck would make three more in his research) provided more than sufficient material for the articles published from October 5–12, 1936, in the *News*. The key thing, and the ethical import, that we notice in these articles is that Steinbeck does not see these people as concepts for a story, but he engages them as a living reality.

The first of these entries begins with the novelistic overview that Steinbeck was perfecting as a trademark:

> At this season of the year, when California's great crops are coming into harvest, the heavy grapes, the prunes, the apples and lettuce and the rapidly maturing cotton, our highways swarm with the migrant workers, that shifting group of nomadic, poverty-stricken harvesters driven by hunger and the threat of hunger from crop to crop, from harvest to harvest, up and down the state....[2]

Both the style and substance of the grammatical structure were to become important hallmarks in Steinbeck's prose. It begins as a periodic sentence, traveling almost like a cinema camera from the general conditions to the specific subject. Once that subject, the migrants, is reached, the sentence turns cumulative, adding detail to our knowledge of the migrants. Significantly, however, this is precisely the way Steinbeck engages the migrants as a people: the general conditions, those caught in the conditions, then individual stories that bring the nature and needs of that people to life. It is not necessary then for the author to cite research data, long quotations by presumed authorities, or statistics. The reader comes to know the people by being there.

The seven articles are carefully focused and divided according to task or category. For example, the first article provides an overview of the migrants, their families, and California's relationship with them. The farmers' needs come

---

[2] John Steinbeck, *The Harvest Gypsies* (Berkeley: Heyday Books, 1988) 19. Future quotations from *The Harvest Gypsies* will be cited parenthetically.

suddenly with the onset of harvest, but the work life of the migrants is contained only by the harvest. Thus an orchard complex might need only 20 year-round employees, but 2,000 harvesters for two weeks. Those harvesters are essential, but only until the harvest is done. In *The Grapes of Wrath* Steinbeck often uses insect imagery for the migrants. Throughout *The Harvest Gypsies* he uses the image of an army. We first meet this force as broken, wandering, and overwhelmed:

> They arrive in California usually having used up every resource to get here, even to the selling of the poor blankets and utensils and tools on the way to buy gasoline. They arrive bewildered and beaten and usually in a state of semi-starvation, with only one necessity to face immediately, and that is to find work at any wage in order that the family may eat.

And there is only one field in California that can receive them. Ineligible for relief, they must become migratory field workers. (20)

Having provided an overview of the problem in the first article, Steinbeck steps into their lives in the second.

To use words that don't appear in Steinbeck's regular vocabulary, he began to see the migrants not as a vast army of the dispossessed, but as living souls, as sacred beings no matter how mean their circumstances. As he reports from one specific squatters' camp, individual humans emerge to life. Here is the engagement. Here resided the reality past the numbers: "Here in the faces of the husband and his wife, you begin to see an expression you will notice on every face; not worry, but absolute terror of the starvation that crowds in against the borders of the camp" (27). In each instance, "Dignity is all gone, and spirit has turned to sullen anger before it dies" (29). In a makeshift tent he discovers:

> There is no bed. Somewhere the family has found a big piece of old carpet. It is on the ground. To go to bed the members of the family lie on the ground and fold the carpet up over them.... The three year old child has a gunny sack tied about his middle for clothing. He has the swollen belly caused by malnutrition. (29)

Several such portraits appear, each accentuating the fact that these are human lives, not dispensable statistics. These are the words of one who practices the ethics of engagement.

Subsequent chapters alternate between such portraits and editorializing on what must be done for the people. In article four, however, Steinbeck reflects upon his frequent use of the word *dignity,* and his fear of the effects when dignity is lost. The passage is significant because it reveals much about Steinbeck's thought regarding the ethics of dignity in *The Grapes of Wrath,* and is, in fact, one of the very few points in his writing where he uses the word:

> In this series the word *dignity* has been used several times. It has been used not as some attitude of self-importance, but simply as a register of a man's responsibility to the community. A man herded about, surrounded by armed guards, starved and forced to live in filth loses his dignity; that is, he loses his valid position in regard to society, and consequently his whole ethics toward society. (39)

If we recall that Steinbeck pictures the migrants as an army, which may be broken and confused at present but can also rise up in anger, we see the germ of the ethical pattern of reciprocity essential to understanding *The Grapes of Wrath.* Left alone to their own devices, excluded from the help of the community (sanitary camps), and marginalized by others, the migrants can vent their distress and overflow in anger. Conversely, bestowing dignity upon the migrants by fair work, meeting their needs, and keeping order in turn make them valuable members of the community.

In the concluding article to the series Steinbeck made the direct appeal that he could only dramatize in the novel:

> The new migrants to California from the dust bowl are here to stay. They are of the best American stock, intelligent, resourceful, and, if given a chance, socially responsible. To attempt to force them into a peonage of starvation and intimidated despair will be unsuccessful. They can be citizens of the highest type, or they can be an army driven by suffering and hatred to take what they need. On their future treatment will depend which course they will be forced to take. (62)

But the point, which he again figures in the army image, is the same. There is an ethics of reciprocity evident in human relations that is essential to all humanity. The bestowal of dignity and respect does not run into an ethical barricade. As Steinbeck sees these people in his own engagement of them, he also sees that dignity and respect will be reciprocated.

Bringing In the Sheaves

In *The Harvest Gypsies* articles Steinbeck established his, and our, basic ethical understanding for *The Grapes of Wrath*. It rests upon two points. First, we are to engage those people we would prefer to shun as living humans, endowed with self-worth and the right to dignity. Second, instead of potential conflict with the migrants, a dubious battle between the haves and have nots, we are to bestow upon them their rightful dignity in ways that restore their human need for a sense of self-worth. Doing so restores a cycle of reciprocity in which our kindness is met by their kindness, our giving to meet needs met by return of that giving. Steinbeck recognizes that this is no easy task. No ethical life is easy. But the alternative he sees, militant class warfare, is always worse, always destructive not only of human life but also of human worth. Into this background a second book, although unpublished at the time, comes into play. *Bringing in the Sheaves*, a purported novel but thinly veiled autobiography by Windsor Drake (Tom Collins), is a story about Steinbeck's work in the migrant camps.

The trip through the San Joaquin Valley with Eric Thomsen served as an arduous introductory tour. They finally arrived at the Acorn Sanitary camps, and there Steinbeck was introduced to the manager, Tom Collins. Collins was the encyclopedia Steinbeck drew upon for *The Grapes of Wrath*. In the foreword that Steinbeck wrote for Collins's manuscript, he begins with a physical portrait of the man:

> The first time I saw Windsor Drake it was evening, and it was raining. I drove into the migrant camp, the wheels of my car throwing muddy water. The lines of sodden, dripping tents stretched away from me in the darkness. The temporary office was crowded with damp men and women, just standing under a roof, and sitting at a littered table was Windsor Drake, a little man in a damp, frayed, white suit. The crowding people looked at him all the time. Just stood and looked at him. He had a small moustache, his graying, black hair stood up on his head like the quills of a frightened porcupine, and his large, dark eyes, tired beyond sleepiness, the kind of tired that won't let you sleep even if you have the time and a bed.[3]

From several years of work with the migrants, Collins knew well their speech patterns, their conventions, their beliefs—all those things that marked them as a unique people. He moved easily among them and on Steinbeck's three subsequent research trips became his invaluable guide. But what was most important, as Jackson J. Benson points out, was this: "It was not

---

[3] Steinbeck, foreword to Windsor Drake (Tom Collins), *Bringing in the Sheaves*, *Journal of Modern Literature* 5.2 (April 1976): 211. Future citations in this chapter will be parenthetical.

only Collins' endurance and capacity for work that attracted Steinbeck's admiration, but his love for people, no matter how poor or how ignorant, and his very large capacity for acceptance."[4] These were lessons Steinbeck himself was to learn.

The value of *Bringing in the Sheaves* resides not only in Steinbeck's foreword, nor in the pragmatic fact that Collins tutored him in the ways of the migrants, but also in the portrait Collins draws of Steinbeck's own involvement.[5] Clearly he was in some awe of the novelist. Clearly also his own prose probably did not merit publication except as an historical artifact. As a book it has no connecting theme; the imagery is turgid; the stories, while moving, haphazardly told. To say that Collins was not a novelist, however, is in no way to diminish its worth as historical artifact. The descriptions of the migrants, their squalid conditions, and Steinbeck's presence among them in their own way shape a powerful story that illumines *The Grapes of Wrath*.

Collins details parts of Steinbeck's sojourn in the camps after his arrival. The account of their tour to the flooded valleys, which appears in the closing chapters of *The Grapes of Wrath*, is especially moving:

> For forty eight hours, and without food or sleep, we worked among the sick and the half starved people, dragging some from under trees to a different sort of shelter, dragging others from torn and ragged tents, floored with inches of water, stagnant water, to the questionable shelter of a higher piece of

---

[4] Benson, "The Background to the Composition of *The Grapes of Wrath*," 57.

[5] According to Benson, who quotes a friend of Steinbeck, Steinbeck returned from his first trip "with 'a pile of material' given him by Collins 'on the Okies and the government camp he managed, with observations and dialogue.'" Ibid., 59.

ground. We couldn't speak to one another because we were too tired, yet we worked together as cogs in an intricate piece of machinery. (221)

Collins paints Steinbeck as a knight in muddy armor:

> I found John lying on his back. He was a mass of mud and slime. His face was a mu[c]ky mask punctuated with eyes, a nose and a mouth. He was close beside me, so I knew it was John. How long we had slept in that mire we knew not. The morning which had hidden its face in shame, had become overburdened with remorse and grief. It shed copious tears, cold, wet, dripping tears that chilled us to the marrow. The long black night, ashamed of its dark deeds, had fled. It fled because it could not face the morning. (222)

Finding a tent with a starving woman and children, Steinbeck set off in the muck and slime and weariness to try to find supplies. Then he returned and "five shrunken bellies consorted with a bite of food—the perfume! And it was a banquet, for a bite of food is a banquet when there is but a bite" (224). Collins's homage lets us see the making of a history as well as a novel.

Unfortunately, that novel was also Collins's undoing. He became known as the man who had introduced Steinbeck to the Okies and manufactured lies. Worse, they were communist lies. He left the Farm Security Administration in 1941, but Steinbeck's acquaintance with him and the experiences he shared with him led directly to chapters 22–26 of *The Grapes of Wrath*.

Working Days

It was not unusual for Steinbeck to keep a journal, notebooks, or a log during his writing, particularly of longer projects. The practice likely started already with *The Long Valley* stories of 1933 and 1934. In the notebooks he kept at the time—lifted from his father's office and crammed margin to margin with his neat but minuscule script—Steinbeck entered story notes, advice to himself, and rough drafts. When he wrote the drafts, the author wrote with what he himself called "sureness of touch." The story came whole and clean, relatively free of emendations, strikeouts, or revision. As Steinbeck approached *The Grapes of Wrath,* the sureness of touch seemed to have deserted him.

Part of this was due to an accretion of events in his increasingly messy personal life. As a rule Steinbeck eschewed the public life of a celebrity, even though the role was being thrust upon him at a dizzying speed. Especially he needed solitude to write, an increasingly scarce commodity. Furthermore, no matter how essential Carol was to his work—she was editor, revisionist, typist, and the one who gave the title to *The Grapes of Wrath*—their marriage had turned brittle and truculent. Then Steinbeck had to contend with his own emotional response to the experiences he had endured. He first approached the writing under the title "The Oklahomans." Nothing is known of this aborted start, although the title suggests an epic sweep. In the opinion of Robert DeMott, based on an interview Steinbeck held with Louis Walther, "The focus of the novel was on the salutary, irrepressible character of the migrants, who, he believed, would profoundly alter the tenor of life in California."[6] The first serious writing took place under the title "L'Affaire Lettuceberg," an angry diatribe that he wrote nearly to its completion before burning the entire manuscript (70,000 words) in early May 1938.[7] He started over,

---

[6] Robert DeMott, introduction to *Working Days: The Journals of* The Grapes of Wrath *1938–1941* (New York: Viking, 1989) xxxvi.

[7] In March 1938, Steinbeck wrote to Elizabeth Otis that "I want to put a tag of shame on the greedy bastards who are responsible for this" (*LL,* 162).

this time with focus upon the migrants, telling the unheard stories of their lives. The entire manuscript was written between June and October 1938. This time, instead of engaging an idea, Steinbeck followed the principle he established in *The Harvest Gypsies* of engaging the migrants themselves.

Unlike Steinbeck's *Journal of the Novel: The* East of Eden *Letters*, Steinbeck's journal for *The Grapes of Wrath* is more of an interior monograph, a vivisection of the author's soul. The former work consists of nearly daily letters to his editor Pascal Covici, often turgid with discussions of myth and symbolism. The latter reveals a writer working—the challenges, the indecisions, the successes where he captured a scene or event just right. While Steinbeck took great pains to remove himself from the narrative of *The Grapes of Wrath, Working Days* is a deeply personal account of the author writing the novel.

Steinbeck introduces his entries as "the diary of a book," and so it was. The reason for the diary was to pace himself, for he wanted "this one to be leisurely." What he meant by that was to keep the writing paced, to control it in order to stay within the five to seven months he contemplated. As a writing journal, the book's primary significance lay in Steinbeck's diagram of his day-to-day plan of execution and final output. As a diary, the work bears value for his commitment to the work, impeded as it was by countless interruptions and disturbances, any one of which could throw a writer off track. For example, his publisher, Covici-Friede, went bankrupt, costing Steinbeck $2,500 in royalties due. When he and Carol had built the Los Gatos house (which Carol designed) several years earlier, the neighborhood was still quiet and open. Then a building boom encroached upon their 1.75 acre spread. Steinbeck laments the racket of hammers and a barking dog that drove him "nuts." Always there were people who wanted to see him. And in September he and Carol, seeking peace and privacy, put a bid in on the 360-acre Biddle ranch, which they succeeded in buying but for which they had to build a new house.

Such matters are important stories behind the book. However, *Working Days* clearly demonstrates his engagement of and commitment to the goals he first established in the Arvin Camp. This appears first in his dedication to creating a work of artistic excellence that would also engage the reader: "This must be a good book. It simply must. I haven't any choice. It must be piling detail on detail until a picture and an experience emerge. Until the whole throbbing thing emerges" (*WD* 25). Steinbeck's determination to make it a "good book" was a part of his artistic creed. By this he meant, generally, fullness and clarity of character, sureness of organic imagery, fidelity to experience, and attention to cause and effect in plot. His reference to "piling up detail" was not as cavalier as it sounds. By this Steinbeck means that telling detail by which a character or scene is brought to life. His determination to write a good book here at the outset (June 10, 1938) is rather sadly echoed by an entry on October 19, 1938, just days before completion:

> I only hope it is some good. I have very grave doubts sometimes. I don't want this to seem hurried. It must be just as slow and measured as the rest but I am sure of one thing—it isn't the great book I had hoped it would be. It's just a run-of-the-mill book. And the awful thing is that it is absolutely the best I can do. (90)

The disconsolate observation must be understood, however, in light of the nearly thorough mental and physical exhaustion he endured as he tried to see it through to the finish.

If commitment to his subject was one part of his ethical engagement, the second lay in his effort to bestow dignity upon the migrants. This aim comports with his advocacy in *The*

Harvest Gypsies articles. Although the journal is "about" the writing of a novel, the idea of an ethics of dignity emerges several times. It may appear in passing advice for writing a scene: "We have to know these people. Know their looks and their nature" (29). But it is especially clear as Steinbeck approaches the concluding chapters, the point where the lives of the Okies are most disorganized and undignified:

> Yesterday the work was short and went over the whole of the book in my head—fixed on the last scene, huge and symbolic, toward which the whole story moves. And that was a good thing, for it was a reunderstanding of the dignity of the effort and the mightiness of the theme. I felt very small and inadequate and incapable but I grew again to love the story which is so much greater than I am. To love and admire the people who are so much stronger and purer and braver than I am. (36)

These few sentences serve well as an example of how Steinbeck himself holds the people in ethical perspective.

The Grapes of Wrath

We sometimes consider the fact that Steinbeck composed *The Grapes of Wrath*, this big, beautiful, sprawling book, over a five-month span and shake our heads in wonder. That constitutes only part of the picture, however. Three years had passed since he first made that trip with Eric Thomsen through the clogged and rainy valleys of southern California. And once he turned Carol's typescript in, it took him nearly a full year to recover physically and psychologically from the ordeal. In the years since its publication the novel has endured nearly every critical approach imaginable, and every reader response possible. Yet, except for its use in a very indeterminate way—as an adjective, for example—scant attention has been paid to the ethical underpinnings of the novel. By this claim, I do not reference the multitude of theological or biblical allusions in the novel. I mean ethics as it has been used thus far in this study—one's rightful duties in and for the community of fellow humans. To examine one such pattern in *The Grapes of Wrath*, we might use the heading of the Ethics of Reciprocity.

The story situates in ethical conflict; that is, we find a clearly defined ethical wrong and an emerging sense of the ethical right. That ethical wrong may be judged according to traditional criteria: the effects for better or worse of one human or group of humans upon the larger community. The specific wrong in this case parallels previous works. The individual or group takes from the larger community to possess wealth, to increase power, and to prevent others from acquiring power. We see this manifested in several ways in *The Grapes of Wrath*.

Tom Joad appears along the road. Caustic and cynical, his creed after four years in McAlester prison is each man for himself. But he finds this creed inadequate for living. He becomes a follower instead of Ma Joad's family of man. Casy too has forsaken community. Formerly led by an unholy spirit outside of man, he attempts to flee his sinful obsessions by wandering in the desert. He has returned when Tom meets him, this time seeking the holy spirit of humanity itself. The landowners and the Bank represent the greatest wrongdoers. Both impersonal entities, they use the migrants to their own ends—profit. But profit isn't the end of it, for they are also soulless entities, uncaring for the lives of the people they use up and spit out like so much waste product. The tractors of the Bank flatten lives along with dwelling places. The handbill scheme is nothing less than a military method to divide and conquer, littering the fields with the hopes of the defeated.

Into this Ma Joad steps as a woman of grace and the herald of a different ethic, one of giving rather than taking. But her giving isn't static. It is dynamic and active, initiating at nearly every step a reciprocal giving by others.

Several examples of her ethical character emerge quickly. When the reader first meets Ma she is preparing dinner for the family. She is the nurturer, the feeder. Pa, followed by Tom and Casy, comes in and announces, "'Ma, there's a coupla fellas jus' come along the road, an' they wonder if we could spare a bite?" Ma's response is immediate, "'Let 'em come.... We got a-plenty." The fact of the matter is that they don't have "a-plenty." They are preparing for a long and arduous journey, selling what they can, and hoarding food. But Ma's instinctive reaction is to give. The same is reinforced by the later event in California where she ladles out the family stew to starving children. There, however, the gesture is met by scorn and hostility. Nonetheless, Ma acts upon her own principles.

A second example appears when the Joads join the Wilsons for dinner by Bethany, Oklahoma. Tom asks their permission to stop and eat. Mr. Wilson smiles and welcomes them. He calls his wife out of their tent and it is clear she is in desperate need herself:

> The tent flaps opened and a wizened woman came out—a face wrinkled as a fig leaf and eyes that seemed to flame in her face, black eyes that seemed to look out of a well of horror. She held herself upright by a tent flap, and the hand holding onto the canvas was a skeleton covered with wrinkled skin. (135)

Yet when she speaks, in a melodious, soft voice, she says, "'Tell 'em welcome.... Tell 'em good and welcome.'" She echoes Ma's earlier words, and as before they settle in to eat together.

The pattern continues. Grampa is sick and worsening by the moment. Sairy Wilson offers their tent for Grampa to lie in. With Grampa dying, Granma orders Casy to pray. He protests. She shrieks at him until he relents. Grampa dies. Ethically this is one of Steinbeck's most poignant and telling scenes. The Joads ask permission to stop; Sairy Wilson accommodates their need. Grampa needs a place to die; again the Wilsons accommodate. Even Casy responds to Granma's imprecations. The Joad family "became a unit" in their moment of need and obligation. Pa calls his appreciation to Ivy Wilson, but Al and Tom reciprocate by fixing their broken-down car. Sairy summarizes, "'We're proud to help. I ain't felt so—safe in a long time. People needs—to help'" (142). Sairy also adroitly summarizes Steinbeck's ethical interests in the book: People needs to help. It is what makes us human—and ethical—beings.

Although the point is emphasized several times in the book, the concluding chapters, as a third example, also respond to and fulfill the first two. The Joads and the Wainwright family share a boxcar, one family to each end, as the rains come. Mrs. Wainwright is helping Ma deliver Rose of Sharon's baby. Pa has to build a dike to keep the water from flooding the boxcar. As the men gather around, one rudely articulates the negative ethics: "'It ain't our baby. We can go'" (439). But as Pa grabs a shovel and starts digging, "Over the men came a fury of work, a fury of battle" (440). At the time of need, the individuals become a unit. Into the night they work, staggering about in the weary darkness, led by the tormented Uncle John.

After the dam breaks by a felled cottonwood limb, Pa staggers into the boxcar, only to find the child stillborn. He has no strength left. As if echoing the Sairy Wilson passage, Mrs. Wainwright tells Ma to get some rest while she sits with Rose of Sharon. At first Ma declines, protesting that she's not tired. The interchange that follows is critical:

> The stout woman smiled. "No need to thank. Ever'body's in the same wagon. S'pose we was down. You'd a give us a han'."
> "Yes," Ma said, "we would."

> "Or anybody."
>
> "Or anybody. Use' to be the fambly was first. It ain't so now. It's anybody. Worse off we get, the more we got to do." (444)

A new unity arises from the primeval ooze of the floodwaters. It is wholly fulfilled in the final transformation of Rose of Sharon, a passage of tender beauty and brutal pathos that Steinbeck planned for weeks.

Notice the steps in this scene and how they cements cement the pattern of reciprocity. First, the sick man has starved himself so that his son might live. He literally laid down his life for his child. Now the man is too ill to be able to eat. The second step is the transference of Ma Joad's spirit to Rose of Sharon:

> "Hush," said Ma. She looked at Pa and Uncle John standing hopelessly gazing at the sick man. She looked at Rose of Sharon huddled in the comfort. Ma's eyes passed Rose of Sharon's eyes, and then came back to them. And the two women looked deep into each other. The girl's breath came short and gasping.
>
> She said "Yes."
>
> Ma smiled. "I knowed you would. I knowed." (453)

Pa and Uncle John, who stood as authorities of the family at the start, are here rendered helpless. And Rose of Sharon, a formerly self-centered and naïve little girl, has adopted Ma's mantle of the family of man.

Steinbeck's ethical thesis emerges, as a good novel should, from within the telling of the story. However, in intercalary chapter 14 Steinbeck uses what he called the "general" chapter to expand upon his theme. The chapter briefly discusses what it means to be human and its answer in the coalescence of "I" to "we." As a consequence of the Bank and landowner's arrogant power, "One man, one family driven from the land; this rusty car creaking along the highway to the west. I lost my land, a single tractor took my land. I am alone and bewildered" (152). But suppose, writes Steinbeck, another family pulls in and pitches a tent nearby:

> Here is the node, you who hate change and fear revolution. Keep these two squatting men apart; make them hate, fear, suspect each other. Here is the anlage of the thing you fear. This is the zygote. For here "I lost my land" is changed; a cell is split and from its splitting grows the thing you hate—"We lost our land." (152)

Not only is that the thing that the single-minded landowners or the corporate banks fear, it also references the fundamental ethical stance of the book. Like the writer himself, one small group engages another. They become known. Their needs are evident and met with small kindnesses that bestow dignity. As those acts are reciprocated this body of humanity grows in dignity and worth.

4

My People Are No People

The primary difficulty with naturalistic ethics lies in its inadequate accounting for wrong, the intentional choice, or evil, the presence of distortion from some ideal within the natural totality. This does not mean that naturalism was some blithe idealism, for the struggle for survival can be a precarious one. Nor does it mean that life is a dark and onerous burden, for nature itself plays melodies of great and vivacious beauty. It does mean, however, that from within the system itself, understanding its own parameters, it is incoherent to speak of wrong or evil. They are words in a foreign tongue.

The peculiarity is that during the 1940s Steinbeck endured personal wrongs that simply didn't fit the philosophy. His greatest blow came on May 7, 1948, when Ed Ricketts died in the path of the Del Monte Express. Steinbeck's marriage to Gwyndolyn Conger shipwrecked nearly from the start in 1943 and went down altogether just a few months after Ricketts died, and a long, deep depression suffused him. In addition his writing suffered. *Cannery Row* accumulated a pile of negative reviews. *The Wayward Bus,* although re-capturing the good humor of his motley crew in *Tortilla Flat,* similarly fell into critical discontent. What he needed, Jackson Benson observed, was "Someone like Carol to tell him, 'This stuff is crap. You better ditch it or start over.' And he was writing very, very fast."[1] It was as if Steinbeck was wandering, like one more amoeba in an aphotic swamp.

The Pearl

While the details of such conflicts as the dissolution of his marriage to Gwyn are properly biographical matters and amply discussed in those biographies we have, the proper subject of this study is the development of Steinbeck's ethical thought as seen in the fiction. Here the 1940s offered a dramatic, transitional work in the novella, *The Pearl.* The germ of the novella first appeared in *The Sea of Cortez,* where Steinbeck relates a local legend—"the Pearl of La Paz." According to Jackson J. Benson, Steinbeck began work on the novella in 1944: "Near the end of November, John began work on *The Pearl,* sitting in his unheated woodshed and writing by kerosene lantern—an echo of days long past" (560). The work didn't go smoothly. On December 8, 1944, he wrote Pat Covici: "I'm still struggling away at The Pearl and it isn't going well" (560). By the end of the month he admitted to a writer's "slump" where he couldn't work. The final draft didn't arrive at Viking until May 1945, right at the time when the largely disdainful reviews of *Cannery Row* were in full force. Its first publication as a whole was in the December 1945 issue of *Woman's Home Companion,* followed by book publication by Viking in November 1947 (nine months after *The Wayward Bus*).

While admiration for *The Pearl* was substantial, critical controversy frothed around its edges: Just what kind of work was this generically? With the passage of time, the novella has acquired a rich variety of critical approaches to that question.[2]

---

[1] Jackson J. Benson, *John Steinbeck, Writer* (New York: Viking Press, 1984) 583. Hereafter quotations will be cited parenthetically.

[2] See, for example, John H. Timmerman, "The Shadow and The Pearl: Jungian Patterns in *The Pearl,*" *The Short Novels of John Steinbeck,* ed.

Less certain is what happens in the work thematically. Upon first reading, it seems very much in step with Steinbeck's naturalistic thought of the 1930s.

At its most immediate, narrative level, the book details the explosive conflict of the civilized world, as Steinbeck uses "civilized" in the Cannery Row trilogy to signify the aggressive power structure of society over an outcast minority. Kino and his small clan on the beach are roughly equivalent to the small clan on Cannery Row encroached upon by the civilized world. Typifying the beach group are family ties, poverty, and dreams of a better life—qualities one observes in all of Steinbeck's outcast minority groups. Typifying the civilized world are hatred for the outcast, some degree of wealth and desire for more, and ignoring human need. The civilized world is a devourer, a monster raking the lives of lesser creatures into its insatiable jaws. Not surprisingly, when Kino finds the pearl, he thinks of it first as a means of access to things of the civilized power structure previously denied him. Just as the larger organism preys upon the lesser, so the smaller organism aspires toward the larger in an evolutionary spiral. Thus far, then, one would see the story in accord with Steinbeck's naturalistic ethics.

In *The Pearl,* the ethical issues arise in a contrast between Juana's Song of the Family and the clangor of greed. The story begins with the song of the family ruling—a clean melody in Kino's mind sanctifying his commonplace life as harmonious and good. It is the *whole.* The whole, however, may be fractured, and Steinbeck names the assailant evil. We see this

---

Jackson J. Benson (Durham: Duke University Press, 1990) 143–61; Harry Morris, "*The Pearl*: Realism and Allegory," *English Journal* 52 (October 1963): 487–95, 505; and Peter Lisca, who draws relationships between the pearl and Mayan mythology in *John Steinbeck: Nature and Myth* (New York: Thomas Y. Crowell, 1978).

first when the scorpion moves down the cradle rope to the sleeping child. In *The Sea of Cortez,* Steinbeck himself might have watched the same scorpion glide surreptitiously toward its prey, a small desert mouse perhaps, and proclaimed it a part of the whole as the stinger barbed home. Here, however, it emerges as the Song of Evil. There is nothing inherently evil in the scorpion itself, but here Steinbeck identifies the threat as "The music of the enemy, of any foe of the family, a savage, secret, dangerous melody..." (5). This is a new ethical vocabulary, designating a trenchant reality against which humans constantly struggle and often lose. It is not part of some cycle of the whole, but an agency, an instinct, a primitive threat embedded within it.

Besides being the vital impulse for the story, the event that establishes Kino's need and the refusal of others to help, the scene is clearly synecdochic for the novella as a whole. Just as Kino crushed the scorpion, so the doctor crushes the family need: "He could kill the doctor more easily than he could talk to him, for all of the doctor's race spoke to all of Kino's race as though they were simple animals" (9). And the doctor confirms the thought, "I am a doctor, not a veterinary" (11). After Kino finds the pearl, the conflict broadens and intensifies.

The novella is clearly one of Steinbeck's short masterpieces of artistry. It is suffused with imagery patterns to abet and intensify the thematic properties. Color imagery, particularly hues of red to convey emotions of anger and confusion and light imagery juxtaposing the brightness of family comfort and the lividity of abandonment and fear play a steady role. Most significant, in accord with how the power structure of civilization holds the needy and unprivileged, is the use of animal imagery. The doctor makes the Indians feel like animals; when Kino finds the pearl, "He put his head back and howled," (20). Perhaps it is with success at this moment, but it is the first step in his devolution to a purely naturalistic state, the struggle for survival, initiated by the evil of a civilization that refuses to recognize his humanity.

The rise of the song of evil and Kino's animalism develop concomitantly: "The music had gone out of Kino's head, but now, thinly, slowly, the melody of the morning, the music of evil, of the enemy sounded..." (27). Kino's security, his protective enclosure, diminishes from the species to the solitary little unit of his family. "Who do you fear?" Juana asks him at one point. His response: "Everyone" (36). And with this recognition, hatred begins to grow in him like a nest of scorpions. He becomes the *isolato,* the single man in a deleterious unit with no one to trust. When he tries to sell the pearl, he "had grown tight and hard. He felt the creeping of fate, the circling of wolves, the hover of vultures. He felt the evil coagulating about him, and he was helpless to protect himself. He heard in his ears the evil music" (50–51). Kino stands helpless and alone, a symbol not only of a solitary Indian youth before the spiteful greed of civilization but also as an emblem of any human struck dumb before powerful forces he cannot control or flee. He is the archetype of Steinbeck's 1940s ethical bewilderment. There is evil out there, vast and implacable, leaving the exposed self humbled and in pain. What one can do about it is less certain.

Juana believes she knows what to do: hurl the pearl back to its source in the sea. She arises in the night. Kino follows, "his brain...red with anger." When he catches her, he "looked down at her and his teeth were bared. He hissed at her like a snake" (59). The evil has insinuated itself into the last remnants of unity, destroying the song of the family itself. And as the evil music fills the night, Kino's transformation into animal grows complete:

> Some ancient thing stirred in Kino. Through his fear of dark and the devils that haunt the night, there came a rush of exhilaration; some animal thing was moving in him so that he was cautious and wary and dangerous; some ancient out of the past of his people was alive in him. (69)

This very thing, erupting redly in Kino now, is domesticated, tamed by the song of the family. But here all the notes are broken, the melody destroyed.

The song returns when Juana insists on going with him on his flight. Her belief in the family is as resilient and powerful as ever. With trackers following, they set out. As Kino tries to surprise the trackers, he discovers that "the song of the family had become as fierce and sharp and feline as the snarl of a female puma" (84). In this case, the female puma is none other than Juana. Fittingly, she stands by Kino's side, her dead Coyotito on her own shoulder, as he looks into the "gray, ulcerous" pearl by the edge of the sea. He offers it to her to throw back. She answers, "No, you." Just as he found the pearl and became obsessed by it, so too it is his task to restore the song of the family by throwing it away.

The Pearl represents a significant development in Steinbeck's ethics by the simple recognition of the presence of evil. At this point, we can assert several things about the nature of that evil. First, it emanates from a certain attitude by which a person or group of persons holds another person or group of persons. To see another as less than human, to prey upon, to take advantage of another, signals a dislocation in the harmony of the species but also in the individual soul. Second, the reason for this disharmony appears as either greed or power. If the lesser group has something desired by the larger, it creates at least the possibility of ethical wrong. To act on that desire is an exercise in evil. Furthermore, because that aggressive group has power, it feels entitled to obtain what it desires. Third, evil isn't manifested in human conflict alone, but also in natural conflict. In the world of *The Pearl,* nature grows red in tooth and claw. We might say that the scorpion that stings Coyotito is benign: that is, it simply does what evolution has designed it to do. But should it be in the hut, involved in human affairs rather than its natural environment? Should it sting Coyotito rather than its natural prey? As Robert Frost reflected in "Design":

> What brought the kindred spider to that height,
> Then steered the white moth thither in the night?
> What but design of darkness to appall?—
> If design govern in a thing as small.
> If by design or naturalistic process, the scorpion too is a small thing but appalls in its disturbing power.

While *The Pearl* provides a keener sense of ethical conflict than *The Sea of Cortez,* especially as it probes the problem of evil, it does not fully satisfy our earlier question: "What is the source of evil?" That is to say that Steinbeck adequately describes the problem of evil, but we are left wondering whether he provides any solution or alternative to it. Since he still operates within a naturalistic philosophy, we have to remove him from issues of theodicy, shared by the three major monotheistic religions—Christianity, Judaism, and Islam. Faced with the conundrum of an all-powerful and all-good God and the reality of evil, a theodicy (*theos,* god, and *dike,* justice) has to demonstrate the justice of God and the presence of evil. Here Steinbeck recognizes the problem, but fails to offer a solution. To throw the pearl back into the sea may absolve Kino's own greed and protect him from the greed of others, but does not solve the problem of greed.

This is not unusual. The Greek philosophers, by and large, were content to recognize evil, reflect on it, and try to explain it. They were categorists. Modern humans are pragmatists. We see evil, identify it, and attempt to resolve it so it will not bother us anymore. If we can't resolve it now, we call it a "mystery" with the suggestion that it will be solved soon. But the pragmatic view is also a defeatist view. Using the three traditional categories by which philosophers have treated evil, we find metaphysical evils first. These are the disruptions endemic to natural processes. They include earthquakes and tsunamis, for example. They might also explain the scorpion gliding down the cradle rope toward Coyotito. Second, we have physical and mental ills, those things that discomfort our lives and ultimately include death. Finally, we have moral evil, by which we mean human wrongdoing, sin, or wickedness. We might say of *The Pearl* that the second and third typify Coyotito and the civilized power bloc respectively.

Here arises the problem for a naturalistic ethics. The crimes perpetrated by the doctor, the pearl traders, the teachers, are crimes. They violate some unnamed standards of human existence that we might, and Plato did, call virtues. We might call their actions sins insofar as they violate the virtues. But "sin" emerges at a state of evolution when humanity is a moral agency, a rational being. There would have been animal behavior and instinct, as Steinbeck's imagery makes clear, but no moral agency. This remained for him to probe in the convoluted passages of *East of Eden*.

East of Eden

The seeds of *East of Eden* were in Steinbeck's mind as early as 1933, when he wrote to George Albee, "I think I would like to write the story of this whole valley, of all the little towns and all the farms and the ranches in the wilder hills. I can see how I would like to do it so that it would be in in the valley of the world. But that will have to be sometime in the future. I would take so very long" (*LL*, p. 73–74). While he took a step toward this in *The Pastures of Heaven*, that "sometime in the future" did not arrive until November 17, 1947, when Steinbeck began to contemplate the actual writing:

> I have a great deal of work to do this year and I would like to get it all done by this summer because then I would like to stop everything to do a long novel that I have been working on the notes of for a long time. It seems to me that for the last few years I have been working on bits and pieces of things without much continuity and I want to get back to a long slow piece of work. I need to go out there for a lot of research so I may be out in California this summer. (*LL*, 301)

To Ed Ricketts a few months later Steinbeck wrote again of his novel-to-be, projecting it at "nearly half a million words" and reminding himself of the need for careful deliberation to get all the words right (*LL*, 309). Finally, in August 1950, he announced to Webster ("Toby") Street that he was nearly ready: "I want to start on my long novel—the one I have been practicing for all my life. It is the Salinas Valley one. I think that if I am not ready to write it now, I never will be. I am nearly fifty and I've been practicing for about 33 years" (*LL*, 408). And the feeling did not relent as he engaged the work. In July 1952, when he was nearly finished with the manuscript, Steinbeck noted: "That earlier work was practice for this, I am sure. The rest was practice."[3]

Of no other work had Steinbeck spoken with such persistent fondness, and several factors account for his feeling. Nearly all of Steinbeck's work arises out of his own peculiar experience, and the stories are of people and places Steinbeck knew. The further Steinbeck moved from this spring of personal

---

[3] John Steinbeck, *Journal of a Novel: The* East of Eden *Letters* (New York: Viking Press, 1969) 117.

experience that nourished his work, the less successful his work was. The strictly cerebral works such as *The Short Reign of Pippin IV* lack the compelling quality that fascinates a reader. *East of Eden* is unique among the works based on Steinbeck's life experience because it is, in part, the story closest to him—his own. And it is the only story in which he enters directly as a character.

Furthermore, its vastness was compelling to him. Instead of being a small slice of life like *Tortilla Flat, Cannery Row,* or *Sweet Thursday,* this work took on the whole life. It contained in practice the theory of *The Log from the Sea of Cortez*—that all life must be seen whole in its environment, in relation to the all. It would bring all the threads together for him. It is no accident that over and over in *Journal of a Novel* he concludes a letter to Covici with this phrase: "I will get to my knitting."

One observes also that the work represented, in moral theme, a response to all his earlier work. For such reasons Steinbeck took unrelenting, pure joy in the writing:

> I have never enjoyed my own work as I have this book. I am as excited about it now as on the day I started it. There is no let down in my energy. I still think it is The Book, as far as I am concerned. Always before I have held something back for later. Nothing is held back here. This is not practice for a future. This is what I have practiced for. (*JN*, 124)

East of Eden was to be the focal point for the moral views about humankind and human relationships that he had been developing since the early thirties.

Although *East of Eden* is quite straightforward in developing its moral theme, the narration itself is fairly convoluted, ranging over families, generations, and locales. All these, however, are strategized to show how a particular ethical code plays out through generations, either to good effects or bad. Here, for the first time, Steinbeck clearly depicts how individual choices affect communities. Not all individuals are mindful of those effects; thus the ethical dialectic of the novel lies between those individuals who choose their own way regardless of community effects and those who choose and act in such a way that safeguards the free choice of others in the community.

As he did so successfully in "The Chrysanthemums," Steinbeck uses the opening paragraphs to establish an image that in turn metaphorically contains the theme of the novel. The first-person narrator nearly becomes omniscient as he beholds the broad expanse of the Salinas Valley where the story will take place. The Valley is gripped between darkness and light:

> I remember that the Gabilan Mountains to the east of the valley were light gay mountains full of sun and loveliness and a kind of invitation, so that you wanted to climb into their warm foothills almost as you want to climb into the lap of a beloved mother. They were beckoning mountains with a brown grass love. The Santa Lucias stood up against the sky to the west and kept the valley from the open sea, and they were dark and brooding—unfriendly and dangerous. I always found in myself a dread of west and a love of east. (*EOE* 3)

So too the characters of the novel are situated between light and dark, between love and dread. Further, the passage sets the ethical imprint between those who dwell in the light by virtue of loving actions and those who dwell in the dark and whom we dread.

The theme is picked up and reinforced at different points in the novel. For example, in chapter 34 the narrator reflects,

> I believe that there is one story in the world, and only one, that has frightened and inspired us, so that we live in a Pearl White serial of continuing thought and wonder. Humans are caught—in their lives, in their thoughts, in their hungers and

> ambitions, in their avarice and cruelty, and in their kindness and generosity too—in a net of good and evil. I think this is the only story we have and that it occurs on all levels of feeling and intelligence. Virtue and vice were warp and woof of our first consciousness, and they will be the fabric of our last, and this despite any changes we may impose on field and river and mountain, on economy and manners. There is no other story. A man, after he has brushed off the dust and chips of his life, will have left only the hard, clean questions: Was it good or was it evil? Have I done well—or ill? (413)

This is the state of our being. As in existentialism, we can't help being there. Although there is no evidence whatsoever that Steinbeck read the major, contemporary existential philosophers, there is at least a fascinating ethical parallel. Furthermore, it is wise to heed the admonition of Joseph Brennan who pointed out that "One trouble with trying to say something about existentialist ethics is that existentialism does not have a great deal of explicit ethical theory."[4] Nonetheless, several basic points might well throw light on *East of Eden*.

To explore this hypothesis at any definitive length, of course, would be self-defeating. Therefore, the focus here will be on an all too brief summary of the basic tenets of existentialism, with primary focus on Martin Heidegger (1889–1976) as the early representative. Heidegger's major work, *Being and Time* (1927), surely influenced such later works as Sartre's *Being and Nothingness* (1953), a work that is in many ways the ethical bookend to Heidegger's phenomenology. The three primary concepts that order Heidegger's system are being, time, and death. All the other terms that have entered our vocabulary through his works are there to support one of these three major points.

---

[4] Joseph Gerard Brennan, *Ethics and Morals* (New York: Harper and Row, 1973) 179.

Heidegger's stated goal is to elucidate the meaning of being.[5] Our error has been to determine being according to natural categories, the model in the western world since Aristotle. But humanity is unique from nature, so, the question becomes, what is it that makes one human? The short answer is *dasein,* a term Heidegger uses in place of *human,* since the word designates existence: *sein-da* is being there.[6] Furthermore, we understand this as living within a situation, a space and time the individual has not created. Basically, *dasein* is Heidegger's structuring of the classic principle of existentialism: existence precedes essence. This too might describe how we meet Samuel and Cathy at the outset of the story.

In Heidegger's thinking, however, existence is never general, but particular. One may only experience one's own existence, but it is experienced in the world and with others.[7] One has two ways of dealing with the world. One is fallenness, a state in which the individual merely follows the commands and will of the world. The other way is by authenticity, the discovery of possibilities for oneself by which one defines oneself as an essence. Humanity, then, is unified by facticity, those things we hold in common. For Heidegger these include, for example, anxiety or a fundamental concern for one's own welfare. Any attempt to grasp our authentic selves creates a threat (anxiety). The ultimate threat, then, is death.

---

[5] Cf. "Being is the most universal and emptiest of concepts. As such it resists every attempt at definition." Martin Heidegger, *Being and Time,* trans. John MacQuarrie and Edward Robins (London: SCM Press, 1962) 2.

[6] Heidegger uses *being* literally in dozens of different ways, from *Etwas-sein* ("being something") to *Alleinsein* ("being alone").

[7] See Heidegger, *Being and Time,* 85: "Being-in-the-world gets its ontological understanding of itself in the first instance from those entities which it itself is *not* but which it encounters 'within' its world, and from the Being which they possess."

Death is the keystone to Heidegger's philosophy. It happens only to one individual, either yourself or not yourself. You may suffer the death of someone else, but you can only experience your own, in your own existence. So, we make a connection here. *Dasein* is the act of making projections for oneself in time.[8] The inauthentic self (facticity), however, avoids the presence of death in time. Death is something that occurs in obituary columns, without personal confrontation. Or, one might project death into the future; death is always not about to happen soon. In Heidegger's thinking, however, an authentic life must always confront death as an imminent possibility. We exist only and continually in relation to death.[9] By confronting death in such a way, we also have the opportunity to see life authentically. The confrontation wrenches one from the tendency to see life as a banal succession of minutes to a view of life as a moment, here and now, as possibility. Such a view, for Heidegger, liberates one from time (hence, Being and Time), since in the confrontation with death we see life as being.

Heidegger clearly proposes a phenomenology and ontology; ethics must be derived by extrapolation. Moreover, his focus is almost exclusively upon the individual action for oneself. Very little is said about positive or just actions toward

---

[8] Ibid., 239: "As something factical, Dasein's projection of itself understandingly is each case already alongside a world that has been discovered. From this world it takes its possibilities."

[9] This belief became a hallmark of later existentialism. See particularly Albert Camus's *The Myth of Sisyphus,* (trans. Justin O'Brien [New York: Vintage Books, 1955]). Camus opens his text thus: "There is but one truly serious philosophical problem, and that is suicide" (3). Camus doesn't mean suicide of others, but of oneself. To answer yes to the question of whether I should commit suicide today is to deny the authenticity of your existence. To answer no is to affirm your existence before, during, and after whatever trials may arise in time.

or in community. Where, then, does ethics arise in existential thinking, and how does it help us further understand our major characters in *East of Eden*? Set aside for a moment two strands of existential thinking: first, the theistic existentialists (Kierkegaard, Berdaev, Shestov, Dostoyevsky) who find spiritual grounding for their ethics, and, second, the idealistic existentialists such as Albert Camus who grounds his ethics in a doctrine of love. That narrows the field, but also in a most logical way, to Jean-Paul Sartre who both followed and qualified elements of Heidegger in *Being and Nothingness*.

To approach Sartre's ethics, though, it is helpful to begin with his most basic proposition. Contrast it with the theistic existentialists, who believe that God precedes humanity and endows it with both existence and essence. Sartre and other atheistic existentialists hold that God does not exist and the only reality is humanity. That is why Sartre says that one is what one conceives oneself to be. His famous definition for humanity—"a plan which is aware of itself"—comes into play here. Furthermore, by dismissing God, Sartre argues that humanity is abandoned from any divine values. Humanity is "condemned to be free."[10] But only by certain means.

Lifting the term directly from Heidegger, Sartre observes that our given situation is facticity. It is the set of facts about one that defines one's situation. A person does not cause these facts; they are, if you will, the accident or situation of one's existing. Moreover, one can do nothing about these facts. One might be 5′3″, whether in high heels or skydiving or climbing Mount Everest. The latter are all situations, not being.

---

[10] See Jean-Paul Sartre, *Being and Nothingness*, trans. Hazel E. Barnes (New York: Philosophical Library, 1956): "I am condemned to exist beyond my essence, beyond the causes and motives of my act. I am condemned to be free" (439). Also, "We are not free to cease being free" (ibid.).

Sartre's phenomenology colors all of his fictional art, but none so brilliantly as the novel *Nausea,* which perfectly exemplifies the argument of *Being and Nothingness. Nausea* follows the diary of Antoine Roquentin, who lives in thorough disgust of his uneventful life. "'I have never had adventures,' he says. 'Things have happened to me.'"[11] His life is empty of event and emotion; he is abandoned to mere existence. Later, still awaiting an adventure, Roquentin observes: "Now I knew: things are entirely what they appear to be—and behind them…there is nothing."[12] Roquentin's words could be Cathy Ames's. Her life has been surfaces.

This is facticity. One cannot change it, but one can transcend it—thus the term *nothingness,* the act of evaluating situations, considering alternatives, and choosing among them. Nothingness is the negation of facticity. Nothingness is an action; it turns from facticity and engages possibilities. By so doing, and by so choosing, one begins to define a self. One seizes one's essence. Thus freedom, for Sartre, a one-time war prisoner, is the essential ethical value. In an uncommitted life, the situation determines the individual—one is what facticity says what one is. But we have freedom to intend, and to choose. This means, then, that one can interpret the world and assign values to it of one's own choosing. This is authentic living. It also gives an ethical system, for if one lives in facticity without exercising free choice, that person is living—in the term Sartre borrowed from Simone de Beauvoir—in "bad faith." It is this same tension between the ethical choice of good and evil that Steinbeck highlights in *East of Eden*. The choice focuses most clearly on the good actions of Samuel and the evil actions of Cathy.

---

[11] Jean-Paul Sartre, *Nausea,* trans. Lloyd Alexander (New York: New Dimensions Press, 1964) 37.

[12] *Ibid.,* 96.

The Light and the Dark

Clearly, the moral juxtaposition between light and dark in *East of Eden* centers on Samuel and Cathy. The thought that affects Samuel's actions most powerfully is summarized in Lee's commentary during their *timshel* discussion: Of the Cain-Abel story, Lee observes,

> I think this is the best-known story in the world because it is everybody's story. I think it is the symbol story of the human soul. I'm feeling my way now—don't jump on me if I'm not clear. The greatest terror a child can have is that he is not loved, and rejection is the hell he fears. I think everyone in the world to a large or small extent has felt rejection. And with rejection comes anger, and with anger some kind of crime in revenge for the rejection, and the crime guilt—and there is the story of mankind. I think that if rejection could be amputated, the human would not be what he is. (270)

It is Samuel's nature to love, not to reject. Even though he involuntarily shivers when he first meets Cathy (172), Samuel was never cruel toward her. When Steinbeck describes the early settlers in the valley, he virtually describes Samuel:

> It is argued that because they believed thoroughly in a just, moral God they could put their faith there and let the smaller securities take care of themselves. But I think that because they trusted themselves and respected themselves as individuals, because they knew beyond doubt that they were valuable and potentially moral units—because of this they could give God their own courage and dignity and then receive it back. (12)

Cathy Ames, on the other hand, is devoid of love, kindness, and trust. In the prelude to chapter 8, the narrator reflects on physical and moral monsters. It is a delicate passage, for the narrator observes that to a monster, the norm must appear monstrous. It is a threat. But what of the moral monster, for it is here that the narrator places Cathy Ames:

> It is my belief that Cathy Ames was born with the tendencies, or lack of them, which drove and forced her all of her life. Some balance wheel was misweighted, some gear out of ratio. She was not like other people, never was from birth. And just as a cripple may learn to utilize his lack so that he becomes more effective in a limited field that the uncrippled, so did Cathy, using her difference, make a painful and bewildering stir in her world. (72–73)

However exquisite Cathy's personal beauty, which the narrator emphasizes here, it is surprising that three dominant, and negative, uses of animal imagery are used for her. Primary among these are cat behavior; snake imagery, suggesting her deceitful nature; and hoof imagery, although used only once, suggesting her diabolical nature. The overriding quality of her moral monstrosity, however, lay in the fact that, like the powers of civilization in *The Pearl*, she used other people:

> Nearly everyone in the world has appetites and impulses, trigger emotions, islands of selfishness, lusts just beneath the surface. And most people either hold such things in check or indulge them secretly. Cathy knew not only these impulses in others but how to use them for her own gain....

Cathy learned when she was very young that sexuality with all its attendant yearnings and pains, jealousies and taboos, is the most disturbing impulse humans have.... Everyone concealed that little hell in himself, while publicly pretending it did not exist—and when he was caught up in it he was completely helpless. Cathy learned that by the manipulation and use of this one part of people she could gain and keep power over nearly anyone. It was at once a weapon and a threat. It was irresistible. And since the blind helplessness seems never to have fallen on Cathy, it is probable that she had very little of the impulse herself and indeed felt a contempt for those who did. (75)

Like Plato, and like Melville, Steinbeck here situates personal, human evil in a monstrous accident at birth.

A revealing side of this nature occurs when Adam visits Cathy as the whore mistress Kate. Here Kate reveals the depth of her hatred for Samuel.

> [Adam] said aloud, "Sam Hamilton has been a good friend to me all the years. I'll miss him."
>
> She had spilled some rum, and it moistened the corners of her mouth. "I hated him," she said. "I would've killed him if I could."
>
> "Why? He was kind to us."
>
> "He looked—he looked into me." (320)

There's the great fear—exposure, and it presages the ending when Kate diminishes physically and psychologically in her darkened room. For Kate, as she admits to Adam, in the whole world "there's only evil and folly" (322). Adam's rejoinder thoroughly exposes Kate's state of soul: "'I know what you hate. You hate something in them you can't understand. You don't hate their evil. You hate the good in them you can't get at. I wonder what you want, what final thing'" (323). The one thing evil people cannot stand is the good in others. They themselves are so removed from the good, the way of Samuel Hamilton's living, for example, that they will seek to destroy it by any means possible. Evil is a succubus, a parasite, looking for something to devour to feed its very nature.

In *Not the Way It's Supposed To Be: A Breviary of Sin*, Cornelius Plantinga Jr., sets himself to the complicated task of determining the nature and workings of sin. His discussion of the parasitical nature of sin might very well be definitive of Cathy Ames. Arguing that "evil always appears in tandem with good," Plantinga explores the actions of evil upon the good.[13] Thus he describes the parasitic nature of sin:

> The reason is that sin is a parasite, an uninvited guest that keeps tapping its host for sustenance. Nothing about sin is its own; all its power, persistence, and plausibility are stolen goods. Sin is not really an entity but a spoiler of entities, not an organism but a leech on organisms. (89)

The worst part of this process is that you can't just kill sin like a poison. It grows immense and complicated root structures that instinctively seek new sources to feed on. Steinbeck posits the conflict as a dualism:

> We have only one story. All novels, all poetry, are built on the never-ending contest in ourselves of good and evil. And it occurs to me that evil must constantly respawn, while good, while virtue, is immortal. Vice has always a new fresh young face, while virtue is venerable as nothing else in the world is. (415)

However eloquent the lines, they strike a new direction in the ethical direction of the novel. Instead of good and evil as accidents of birth, they now exist in tension within one person. This change Steinbeck defends in his ethical creed of "Thou mayest."

The Ethics of Choice

Few specific points in Steinbeck's work have attracted quite the attention that the *timshel* doctrine has. First, Lee lays out the background context of the elderly Chinese intellectuals learning Hebrew to construe the early chapters of the Old Testament. They stumbled over Genesis 4:7, a passage that defines human relationships to sin. The problem arose with

---

[13] Cornelius Plantinga Jr., *Not the Way It's Supposed To Be: A Breviary of Sin* (Grand Rapids: Wm. B. Eerdmans, 1995) 80.

construing the mood of the verb. The American Standard Version uses the imperative form: "If you do not do well, sin is crouching at the door; and its desire is for you, but *you must* master it." The King James Version uses the future imperative mood: "If thou doest not well, sin lieth at the door. And unto thee shall be his [sin] desire, and *thou shalt* rule over him." In both instances, several items seem to have bothered the Chinese scholars. First, in both the orders appear as divine mandates—God to man. Such a view contradicts their Confucian beliefs, which move essentially from human to divine. Second, and consequentially, free human choice appears to be eliminated. Thus they sought to rectify the apparent contradiction by translating the Hebrew verb in the optative case—thou mayest. Signifying choice or desire, this use returns the decision to humanity. Each person has the freedom to choose over sin, which Lee also defines in Confucian terms as ignorance. Lee exults in the discovery:

> "Now, there are many millions in their sects and churches who feel the order, 'Do thou,' and throw their weight into obedience. And there are millions more who feel predestination in 'Thou shalt.' Nothing they may do can interfere with what will be. But 'Thou mayest'! Why, that makes man great, that gives him stature with the gods, for in his weakness and his filth and his murder of his brother he has still the great choice. He can choose his course and fight it through and win." Lee's voice was a chant of triumph. (303)

Samuel shares his exuberance.

Here also emerge problems with the ethics of choice. Consider several points. First, as the existentialists argued, it would appear that Steinbeck agrees that the choices one makes determine or authenticate one's being. The primary criterion for the existentialist in determining the ethical goodness of the choice is whether it in fact benefits my determination of self.

Only secondarily does one question whether it is beneficial or detrimental to community. In broad respects, Steinbeck would appear to be in accord with this belief. However, as we have traced the development of his ethics thus far, we have seen a decided turn toward the wellbeing of the community. This is accentuated in *East of Eden*. Kate's tawdry collection of compromising photographs is wrong because she personally violated trust by choosing to take them and because the photographs directly threaten the harmony of the community at large. As such, she warrants the same degree of vilification as the doctor or the pearl dealers in *The Pearl*.

Within the text itself, secondly, a contradiction in ethical positioning appears. In the tradition of Plato and Melville, as was discussed earlier, Steinbeck describes Cathy as a monster, an aberration at birth. Hers is not simply a propensity toward evil, nor a capacity for evil, but a decided twist at the core of her nature that turned toward evil at every opportunity. The problem then is that Cathy cannot be said to have freedom of choice. Because of her nature she will always choose the wrong thing, and throughout the novel she consistently does choose the wrong thing. In Steinbeck's ethics, where a good choice is one that benefits the individual and the community, Cathy chooses in such a way as to destroy herself and community. She cannot do otherwise given Steinbeck's own premises in the novel.

The contradiction is not resolved in *East of Eden*. If we can extrapolate into a larger ethical arena, which any good novel should permit us to do, we see three options for dealing with a Cathy Ames. One is represented by Samuel Hamilton, whereby we regard her with pity and sadness but offer no direct response. A second option is represented by Adam, who confronts and names the evil. Ultimately, for Adam or ourselves, this is a process of recognition of the wrong and extricating ourselves from it in an attempt at personal liberation. The third option is to leave evil alone to its parasitic nature. Ultimately, according to Steinbeck, evil has no creative force; it is parasitic. Without a host it dies. This is precisely the state of the shrunken, arthritic Kate in her darkened room.

We notice that all these positions are taken by different characters in relation to Cathy. Only they, to resolve the contradiction, have the privilege of "thou mayest," or free choice. It is neither a birthright nor a virtue they have earned. They are all flawed in their own way. It is their privilege because they live in communal welfare with others and refuse to set themselves over the rights of others. To them belongs freedom of choice. But not to Cathy Ames.

If ethics is concerned with individual responsibility and communal justice, then we can trace a clear trajectory in Steinbeck's ethical beliefs through the early 1950s. His early ethics are firmly rooted in naturalist thinking and Darwinian biology. Without a transcendent being responsible for providing a code of ethics for his creation, and without that being's involvement in his creation, life, of which humanity is one part, must follow the principles of survival, protection, and reproduction. An act is right or wrong only as it corresponds to one of these three principles. For example, stealing another's food is an ethical wrong for it denies another's chances of survival, whereas giving of what you have, as with Rose of Sharon breastfeeding the starving man, is an ethical good. To a certain extent, these fundamental principles endure through the early 1950s. For example, Cathy's suicide, even though the necessary end for her narrowing life, is ethically wrong because it denies all three principles.

While not forsaking his essential naturalist views, in the late 1930s and early 1940s Steinbeck began to define more clearly an agency of evil or wrong. This was manifested in the huge, nameless conglomerate of *The Grapes of Wrath* and in more particular agents such as the doctor and the pearl buyers in *The Pearl*. In *The Pearl* also, however, these two are really simply manifestations of the larger civilization—the power bloc that operates by greed and demands—encroaching upon the freedom of the individual. This conflict becomes the centerpiece of *Cannery Row* (1945). Here Steinbeck draws a contrast between the superficial calm and beauty of the tidal pool, but then it darkens as we look below the surfaces. With a jarring description of that shadowed life, Steinbeck writes:

> Here a crab tears a leg from his brother. The anemones expand like soft and brilliant flowers, inviting any tired and perplexed animal to lie for a moment in their arms, and when some small crab or little tide-pool Johnnie accepts the green and purple invitation, the petals whip in, the stinging cells shoot tiny narcotic needles into the prey and it grows weak and perhaps sleepy while the searing caustic digestive acids melt its body down. (13)

As the description continues, Steinbeck appropriates human qualities of evil to describe the ocean life:

> Then the creeping murderer, the octopus, steals out, slowly, softly, moving like a gray mist, pretending now to be a bit of weed, now a rock, now a lump of decaying meat while its evil goat eyes watch coldly. It oozes and flows toward a feeding crab, and as it comes close its yellow eyes burn and its body turns rosy with the pulsing color of anticipation and rage. Then suddenly it runs lightly on the tips of its arms, as ferociously as a charging cat. It leaps savagely on the crab, there is a puff of black fluid, and the struggling mass is obscured in the sepia cloud while the octopus murders the crab. (31)

The analogy between the violence of sea life and civilization is chilling.

Even more chilling is the transition from this vague, amorphous evil called *civilization,* that force that oppresses lesser individuals, the powerless, for its own gain, to this same wrong in human individuals. That is the state in *East of Eden.* Individual humans do wrong, whether from aberrant nature or willful choices. Those people do wrong because their actions damage community. The dignitaries who visit Kate's whorehouse, in Steinbeck's canon of beliefs, are doing no wrong. They are paying for a service that the prostitutes willingly provide and benefit from. Kate's extortion of these same dignitaries through her collection of photographs is wrong because a contractual agreement of payment for services rendered violates the dignitaries' rights and destroys a communal harmony. Her reasons for so doing are the same as the monster civilization—to acquire power over the preyed upon. Thereby she stands at the nadir of Steinbeck's evolving ethics of right and wrong.

5

Heart of Darkness: Light of Heaven

The Winter of Our Discontent is certainly Steinbeck's most divisive book, both in ethical and artistic terms. In her comparison of Steinbeck and Viktor Frankl, Barbara A. Heavilin argues that both believe that "self-absorption is a national sickness."[1] Withdrawing from society to pursue one's own interests results in the "existential vacuum—a psychic emptiness brought on by a lack of a sense of meaning."[2] "Trapped inside of himself," Heavilin adds, "Ethan [Hawley] manifests the emptiness and lack of meaning in life that characterize the existential vacuum."[3] In our earlier discussion of existential ethics, we would have to say, then, that Hawley lives in "bad faith." He severs himself from community; his actions are random and self-serving rather than commitments.

Stephen K. George takes a slightly different approach by studying Hawley's gradual loss of morals; fundamentally he is a good man turned bad. If integrity, as George argues, is the ability to hold fast to certain values, even in the face of adversity, then Hawley is one who simply capitulates, thus forsaking his integrity. By citing certain prominent ethicists,

---

[1] Barbara Heavilin, "The Existential Vacuum and Ethan Hawley: John Steinbeck's Moral Philosophy," *The Moral Philosophy of John Steinbeck*, ed. Stephen K. George (Lantham: Scarecrow Press: 2005) 50.

[2] Ibid.

[3] Ibid., 51.

George further defines integrity as "'self-detachment' in order to accurately assess his or her desires, as well as the moral situation at hand."[4] Furthermore, citing Lynne McFall, George advances the idea that

> Some commitments are so essential to our concepts of our "selves" that to break them would mean "self-betrayal and personal disintegration" because they comprise our "core" and make "us who we are." Without adherence to such essential commitments "we could not 'live with' ourselves; we would not be the persons we thought we were." It is here, in the realm of personal identity, that the concepts of lack of integrity and loss of self-respect meet. The person without integrity inevitably ends up identifying with conflicting desires, thus thwarting any consistent sense of identity. Indeed, lack of integrity "means the mutual undermining of identifications" so that the weak-willed or hypocritical or self-deceived individual eventually has no set of core values or commitments to identify with.[5]

The problem with such an ethical stance, as George points out, is that life necessarily reduces to relativism. Eschewing normative guidelines of community, the individual places himself in the stead of these guidelines. George comments:

> This denial of any ultimate or metaphysical existence of good and evil, virtue and vice, underlies Ethan's naturalistic world view and his subsequent loss of integrity, a virtue that by definition depends on more permanent values and commitments for it to have any meaning.

---

[4] George, "The Disintegration of a Man," 170. See Gabriele Taylor, *Pride, Shame, and Guilt: Emotions of Self-assessment* (Oxford: Oxford University Press, 1985).

[5] George, "The Disintegration of a Man," 70. See Lynne McFall, "Integrity," *Ethics* 98 (1987): 5–20. McFall writes: "A person of integrity is willing to bear the consequences of her convictions, even when this is difficult, that is, when the consequences are unpleasant" (9).

Moreover, just as relativity can justify rationalizations, even becoming the ultimate rationalization for depravity...so do the brutal consequences of rationalizations serve to support relativity.... Furthermore, out of Ethan's conversion to relativity and his comforting self-deceptions comes the third element of his fall, which may have been there all along as an instrumental element in his acceptance of extreme ethical relativity. This third element is Ethan's new willingness to test the moral limits by mentally toying with ideas and conduct that before would have been unthinkable—a sort of recreation with morality (or immorality) that eventually bridges the gap between his inner change and his outer behavior.[6]

Such an ethical stance George aptly calls a perverse "recreation," in which morals are merely playthings.

If this is the case, it signals a growing departure from Steinbeck's earlier ethical stance. While in *East of Eden* Steinbeck created an agency of evil in human nature, in *Winter of Our Discontent* he demonstrates the effects of a broken, and positive, ethical virtue—commitment. Hawley, with the exception of his plagiarized essay, does not so much act in evil desires, thereby harming community, as he lapses into a morose inaction and isolation—thus Heavilin's "existential vacuum."

Standing alongside *East of Eden*, the novel also places us at the heart of the ethical conundrum of interested versus disinterested actions. Cathy Ames represents the interested pole; that is, she uses people and things to satisfy her own desires and ends. Samuel Hamilton represents the disinterested pole; that is, he sets his own interests aside to form a holistic view of the wellbeing of others. By extension, we might say that Ethan Hawley drops in the middle to the murky bog of the uninterested. His sordid little life passes before us without

---

[6] George, "The Disintegration of a Man," 176–77.

light, without commitment or significant action, and virtually without meaning.

Ethan Hawley and Obligations

Clearly for such reasons—his lack of positive commitments, his loss of integrity, his uninterested stance toward life—Hawley represents a negative example in the novel. Therefore, we might say that Steinbeck, as he did in *East of Eden* with Cathy, presents a negative example of a way we should not go. Essentially, in *The Winter of Our Discontent*, Steinbeck draws a *via negativa* in Hawley. This is the way we should not go. But as it is used philosophically, by Thomas Aquinas for example, the *via negativa* is used to arrive at some positive principle or conclusion. We remind ourselves of the proper consideration of the field of ethics stipulated earlier. Not all human actions are ethical concerns. Not all freely chosen actions are ethical concerns. As George Thomas White Patrick, one of the fathers of modern philosophical inquiry put it: "Only the voluntary conduct of rational human beings considered in respect to its *worth* in leading to a certain *end* are ethical concerns."[7] We add that such actions take place by an individual in community with others. Therefore, we conclude that an individual has a certain duty to others. Ethical duties are those established by the laws or norms of the community for the wellbeing of the community. So that certain services may be provided for the community, representatives levy taxes. These same representatives may create laws so that individuals may live at peace in the community. These duties are external to the individual, established for communal harmony.

One may not be inclined to duty, preferring a simple life or the life of a recluse, but to ignore the need of others in

[7] George Thomas White Patrick, *Introduction to Philosophy* (Boston: Houghton Mifflin, 1924) 405.

community constitutes an ethical flaw. If, for example, I see my neighbor working in his yard on a daily basis, then one day see him lying prone in his garden, I fail a duty to him if I don't inquire about his wellbeing. Shutting the drapes is no better. If someone—say the mailman—later finds the man's corpse the garden, I am not exonerated by having closed my drapes. Such an ethical flaw arises from a breach in the sense of obligation, or the deontological ethic that holds that each individual has an obligation to the wellbeing of others. While duty compels us to act in a certain way, the deontological ethic, which we will discuss later, posits an innate sense of obligation. To ignore the man in the garden, even though I have no legal obligation to him (I was not the means of his death), is nonetheless an ethical wrong.

Hawley forswears all such obligations, other than to himself. Traditional norms are targets to be shot down, jokes to smirk at, fantasies unobtainable and not worth pursuing in any event. It is an ethics of abdication. Steinbeck's aim in the novel may have been to dramatize the moral dereliction of the present age. However, in his *via negativa* he appears to offer no legitimate alternative. If this is wrong for such-and-such reasons, an attentive audience has the privilege to inquire *what then is right*? Ethan Hawley falls, but where does he fall from? Such questions, and they are important ones, are not clearly answered in the novel.

In writing the novel it appears that Steinbeck saw himself as a physician, probing a sick and dying body called civilization and trying to determine an etiology for its disease. As we see in the many letters he wrote at the time, he believed he found it. Before actually starting the novel (likely March 1960) Steinbeck was already pondering the theme: a deep sense of loss—of moral fiber, of battling for a way of life, even of loss of moral fortitude. Shortly after Christmas 1959, while he was recovering from his apparent coronary attack at Sag Harbor, Steinbeck wrote Elizabeth Otis:

> True things gradually disappeared and shiny easy things took their place. I brought the writing outside, like a cook flipping hot cakes in a window. And it should never have come outside. The fact that I had encouragement is no excuse. That same cook in a window can draw a crowd too but he is still making hotcakes. I tell you this because if I am able to go back, the first efforts will be as painful as those of a child learning to balance one block on top of another. I'll have to learn all over again about true things. (*LL*, 657)

During the writing of the novel in the spring and summer 1960, Steinbeck provided a number of explanations for its writing. To Pascal Covici on July 1, 1960, he wrote:

> This is an egocentric letter but I thought you might like to know these things. You say it isn't a novel. Maybe you're right. It's not a novel like any I have seen or read or heard of, but as far as I know a novel is a piece of fiction having form direction and rhythm as well as intent. At worst it should amuse, at half-staff move to emotion and at best illuminate. And I can't know whether this will do any of those things but its intention is the third. (*LL*, 676–77)

The source for this goal to "illuminate" had already emerged from his incipient work on Malory.

Increasingly, Steinbeck saw Camelot as a shimmering beacon of moral rectitude in a world blasted and darkened by moral perfidy. In a letter to Elizabeth Otis and Chase Horton, dated March 14, 1958, Steinbeck wrote,

> But the writer of the Morte did not know what had happened, what was happening, not what was going to happen. He was caught as we are now. In forlornness.... And out of this devilish welter of change—so like the one today—he tried to

> create a world of order, a world of virtue governed by forces familiar to him. (*LL*, 576)

In subsequent letters, Steinbeck developed the link between Malory and our age:

> The values have got crossed up. Courtesy is confused with weakness and emotion with sentimentality. We want to be tough guys and forget that the toughest guys were always the wholest guys. Achilles wept like a baby over Patroclus and Hector's guts turned to water with fear. But cleverness has taken the place of feeling, and cleverness is nearly always an evasion. (*LL*, 631)

He also recognized that heroism in the present age, unless offered as a sop to feelings in romantic novels, had become simply anachronistic:

> The hero is almost bad form unless he is in a western. Tragedy—true tragedy—is laughable unless it happens in a flat in Brooklyn. Kings, Gods and Heroes—Maybe their day is over, but I can't believe it. Maybe because I don't want to believe it. In this country [England] I am surrounded by the works of heroes right back to man's first entrance. And if all of this is gone, I've missed the boat somewhere. And that could easily be. (*LL*, 635)

Finally, the link between *Morte D'Arthur* and *Winter* is made clear in a letter to Joseph Bryan of September 28, 1959:

> This has been a good time—maybe the best we have ever have—not wasted at all. But my subject gets huger and more difficult all the time. It isn't fairy stories. It has to do with morals. Arthur must awaken not by any means only to repel the enemy from without, but particularly the enemy inside. Immorality is what is destroying us, public immorality. The failure of man toward men, the selfishness that puts making a buck more important than the common weal. (LL, 649)

Now, next to our own time the 15th century was the most immoral time we know. Authority was gone. The church split, the monarchy without authority and manorial order disappearing. It is my theory that Malory was deploring this by bringing back Arthur and a time when such things were not so. A man must write about his *own* time no matter what symbols he uses. And I have not found my symbols nor my form (*LL*, 649–50)

That last line is telling; for in *The Winter of Our Discontent*, Steinbeck is adept at showing the ethical wrong. He had not yet discovered a symbolic structure by which to oppose that wrong.

Artistic Merit

While the personal motivations for the composition of the novel seem relatively clear, insofar as the letters bear evidence, the author's intentions don't always parallel the reader's perceptions. Most critics are quite settled in their opinion that *The Winter of Our Discontent* ranks low in terms of Steinbeck's artistic abilities. While recognizing certain excellences in the novel, Howard Levant asserts that

> *The Winter of Our Discontent* does not jell as a novel. The expansion of the crisply objective short story produces a sermonic platform, an essayish, mechanical, finally incoherent parable. The novel's failure is due, in part, to the point of view and in part to a lack of conviction in the materials—which are petty in detail, querulous in tone, and thoroughly ambiguous in their fictive embodiment. Perhaps the failure is the revenge of actuality on the author's overly bleak selection of particular

> details. More immediately, the failure is a direct consequence of Steinbeck's mature practice as a novelist.[8]

For Levant, the novel fails artistically because it fails to organize into a whole, a piece where every bit is necessary and contributing to the whole.

Levant refers to "the crisply objective short story" that resides as background for the novel. The reference is to "How Mr. Hogan Robbed a Bank," which appeared, shortly after he composed it, in *The Atlantic Monthly* of March 1956. Specific qualities borrowed from the story for use in the novel are discussed by Warren French in his essay "Steinbeck's Winter Tale." It did not work, according to French. The sum of the borrowing was that "a delightful comic fantasy has been turned into contrived melodrama."[9]

While Howard Levant argues the lack of organizational unity in the novel, and Warren French focuses on the failed transition from short story to novel, Thomas Kiernan sees the novel arising from Steinbeck's own recollections of a simpler and more optimistic youth and his growing awareness of his own financial success in an age of greed:

> In achieving financial security, in aspiring to wide social and political personal acceptance and achieving it, in settling comfortably into the sophisticated and often artificial living environment that was New York—all things that he had formerly professed little interest in—he had betrayed his own fiery artistic principles. The original fire had been reduced to barely glowing embers. As in a self-fulfilling prophecy, the world had forced him, like the Henry Morgan of his first book, to compromise his youthful ideas in order to live comfortably

[8] Howard Levant, *The Novels of John Steinbeck: A Critical Study* (Columbia: University of Missouri Press, 1974) 289.

[9] Warren French, "Steinbeck's Winter Tale," *Modern Fiction Studies* 11.1 (Spring 1965): 66.

> in it. But he was unable to accept the fact that he had unwittingly sold out, that the world had humbled him. Instead he turned his vision of the world around. It was now possible to live in the world and still retain the ideals and hope of childhood.[10]

Therefore, for Kiernan the novel is something of a lamentation of things past. And they are irrevocably past, destroyed in the morass of humanity's darkening spirit of greed.

None of these three views, however, adequately addresses the novel's most apparent failure; that is, as a work of art. It is a picture without lines, causes as events. In a disturbing way, it fulfills the dictum of *The Log from the Sea of Cortez*—"It Might be so"—or Adam's discovery in *East of Eden*—"Thou mayest." But quality in a work of art—aesthetically pleasing because of harmony of the parts, excellence in mastering the medium, creative in execution, and striking in its totality—requires certain recognizable restraints. In his best work, *The Grapes of Wrath*, for example, Steinbeck wove the mood and theme of the story with perfectly coherent telling. The result is a masterpiece. *The Winter of Our Discontent*, on the other hand, is virtually paralyzed by its awkward telling. Steinbeck is less the storyteller and more the philosopher. He is less the intercessory priest of fiction, mediating audience and truth by story, and more the schooled pastor, arguing the way one should not go.

Most immediately noticeable as a change in artistic technique is the startling difference in dialogue. In no other novel had Steinbeck relied so extensively on dialogue to form character and develop plot. He seems to be writing consciously in the modern trend toward quicker action punctuated by dialogue and a dramatic sense of character, a trend patterned

---

[10] Thomas Kiernan, *The Intricate Music: A Biography of John Steinbeck* (Boston: Little, Brown and Co., 1979) 308.

more on television than on the stage. While Steinbeck had a fine-tuned ear for both colloquialism and the rhythm of human speech, revealed at its best in *The Grapes of Wrath* and the Cannery Row trilogy, he is less successful in imitating the dialogue of the faster-paced, rather flippant characters an artist hears whispering at the back of his mind when he sits down to work. They always seem to be strangers to Steinbeck, and while he imitates their slightly foreign speech fairly well, it always bears the mark of the stranger—the one who has to hold up a tape recorder to get it right.

Two specific problems emerge as a result of this heavy emphasis on a dialogue with which Steinbeck was neither wholly at ease nor wholly familiar. First, too often the characters merely pose; they make stage talk to fill lapses in action. They seem to be under the floodlights without a well-rehearsed script, wondering, "Now, what shall we say to fill in two blank pages and make people listen?" Thus we get scenes in which Hawley talks to his vegetable cans or tries hard to make witty remarks that might lift a listener's eyebrow. The second problem arises from the idiosyncratic language Steinbeck uses to distinguish his characters as personalities. Strange little phrases come from the actors' tongues, phrases that emanate from Steinbeck's mind and not from any dramatic necessity of scene or conflict. Many of these are the unusual endearments that also flawed *Burning Bright*: "Good stuff, fern tip"; "Okay, bugflower"; "Yes dearling"; "I won't, my fair, my lovely"; "I bring you tidings of great joy, my flying squirrel"; "I think I'll burn him up, heaven wife"; "they're the first—the very first, my creamy fowl"; "Pigeonflake, I'm going to be a little late." It is certain that Steinbeck would refrain from such maudlin language in his own life. Elaine Steinbeck had her own assessment:

> John was very sparing in his use of such words. When he said—very often to a child—"Dear, I want you to do such and such," it absolutely, always, broke my heart. "Dear" shouldn't be that passionate. He would say it to Gadg [Elia Kazan] in a moment of excitement or of argument, and he'd say, "Now look, dear, I think you are terribly wrong about that" or something like that. And he said it to me, and it always touched me tremendously. But on the other hand, he used all kinds of funny endearments, constantly, and he thought that was his way of showing affection, light affection. So he used it in his books, and it is cloying to most people.[11]

The profligate use of such words in *The Winter of Our Discontent* suggests a forced artificiality. It has long been argued among philosophers of aesthetics whether sincerity is an artistic virtue. Without attempting to respond to the specific issue, it may be said that artificiality, in the sense of contrived and misleading effects, is nearly always an aesthetic flaw. It is in this instance.

We might say, then, that the darkness of the moral stage, the steady deterioration of the central character from an ethical point of neutrality to wrong, and the frequent artificiality of prose mark the novel as flawed. That may be so, but it is also strangely fitting to Steinbeck's ethical development to this point. In *East of Eden* and *The Winter of Our Discontent* Steinbeck has effectively depicted an ethical *via negativa*, a way we should not go. That the latter erupts into condemnation is, perhaps, understandable. Nonetheless, it remained for him now to find a restorative way. For this Steinbeck had to undertake his own attempt to discover restoration. This occurred in his trip to discover the heart of America in *Travels with Charley*.

---

[11] Jackson J. Benson, *The True Adventures of John Steinbeck, Writer* (New York: Viking, 1984) 873.

Travels with Charley

Exposing the ethical wrong is both a philosophical and artistic challenge. Whether Steinbeck met the challenge in *The Winter of Our Discontent* is debatable. Discovering the ethical good is fully as daunting a challenge. Perhaps it took a trip across America to find it. If Steinbeck's disenchantment with American values was not clear enough in *The Winter of Our Discontent,* he reprised many of the same themes in his letters of the time.

Coupled with his work on the Arthurian translation and the inevitable moral parallels he discerned between the lost glory of Camelot and the present-day darkness was a second impulse deriving from his extensive travel abroad. His relentless traveling in the late fifties seemed to distance him from America and to make objective his vision of its people. What he saw from abroad he did not always like or admire. This culminated in his infamous letter to Adlai Stevenson on November 5, 1959, in which he excoriated American greed and moral torpor in much the same voice he used to chastise the "tigers" of civilization lurking outside Cannery Row. Distinguishing between two kinds of Christmases, the one filled with love and sacrifice and the other addled with greed, Steinbeck wrote,

> Well, it seems to me that America now is like that second kind of Christmas. Having too many THINGS they spend their hours and money on the couch searching for a soul. A strange species we are. We can stand anything God and Nature can throw at us save only plenty. If I wanted to destroy a nation, I would give it too much and I would have it on its knees, miserable, greedy and sick. (*LL*, 652)

With such thoughts, *Travels with Charley* became both a flight from and a quest for replacement of those things left behind.

Ethically, the issue becomes this: what enduring virtues may we say are good for all persons and all times? The question has been raised since the birth of the Hebrew nation theologically and since Plato philosophically. For Plato we must follow our reasoning to arrive at our answers; emotions will not do.[12] The highest value is the state—understandably so if we recall from *The Republic* that the state represents and constitutes order in society. The state is a living body as well as a means of order. Plato's *Crito* details the ethical positioning of the individual living in the state, structured upon three primary points. First, we ought not harm anyone. If Socrates were to escape the state, he would violate its laws and therefore harm the state. Second, if one lives in the state when one could in fact flee from it, one is agreeing to live by its laws. If Socrates escaped, he would be breaking an agreement. Finally, the state—in Socrates' system—stands for one's teacher or parent, and one ought to obey one's parents. Notice that all three reasons come with ought-clauses. We might be rightly concerned about the conflict between these and Socrates' insistence upon reason. William Frankena addresses this:

> In each of these arguments Socrates appeals to a general moral rule or principle which, upon reflection, he and his friend Crito accept as valid: (1) that we ought never to harm anyone, (2) that we ought to keep our promises, and (3) that we ought to obey or respect our parents and teachers. In each case he also uses another premise which involves a statement of fact and

[12] The modern philosopher Bernard Gert denies both emotions and "attitudes" as determinative of ethics. These are both egocentric. For Gert, "Moral attitudes, judgments, feelings, etc. must involve people who count as moral agents" (13). Agency, then, how we act on emotions, beliefs, etc., is the determinative quality of ethics. Gert's positioning is somewhat similar to Plato's in that he believes the adequate capacity for right actions resides in human reason. See Bernard Gert, *Morality: A New Justification of the Moral Rules* (New York: Oxford University Press, 1988).

> applies the rule or principle to the case in hand: (1a) if I escape I will do harm to society, (2a) if I escape I will be breaking a promise, (3a) if I escape I will be disobeying my parent and teacher. Then he draws a conclusion about what he should do in his particular situation. This is a typical pattern of reasoning in moral matters and is nicely illustrated here.[13]

Steinbeck's quest was in part an escape; it was nonetheless a flight toward something. He sought nothing less than a discovery of virtue.

The ethical good, however, is not just the avoidance of wrong or harmful actions. If we remember the argument of chapter 1, ethics is concerned with willful acts committed in community. In the case of *Travels with Charley*, Steinbeck did not consider such acts in one isolated community, as he did in his novels, but against the backdrop of the entire nation. Comparing this current trip to his investigative reporting for the *San Francisco News* on the dismal plight of the migrants during the 1930s, Steinbeck observed that he had ceased to "feel" America, to let the reality seep into him through experience rather than through newspapers and books—thus the cause of the quest.

Given his premises, the quest wasn't for virtues primarily. They came secondarily, from the events encountered on the journey. In fact, at the close of his journey he returns once more to his premise and reflects: "The more I inspected this American image, the less sure I became of what it is" (216). Yet, Steinbeck did find an abundance of good people and good deeds that ameliorated the essentially dyspeptic view of *The Winter of Our Discontent*. Since this exquisite travel narrative, which ranks among his top works in pure craftsmanship, is episodic, it would do the work a disservice to reduce it to a list

---

[13] William K. Frankena, *Ethics* (Englewood Cliffs: Prentice-Hall, 1973) 2.

of points or lessons learned. Instead, the reader has to "feel" the episodes as Steinbeck did, assimilating them into a mosaic effect. Lamenting the terrific and tangled pace of modern life, Steinbeck observes that "we hadn't had time to develop the means to think, for man has to have feelings and then words before he can come close to thought and, in the past at least, that has taken a long time" (31). In Steinbeck's case, the "long time" was the long and winding road he took in Rocinante. To feel America, then, whether by Steinbeck's experience or by engaging the book, means two things. First, it means actual experience, and second, it means reflection on the experience. There is the trip, and there is the story of the trip.

In the text, even with its essentially episodic character, Steinbeck appears to find ways in which the nation's stories may be felt. Some of them appear to be ethically ambivalent, perhaps more similar to non-teleological is-thinking encounters of *The Log from the Sea of Cortez*. From other stories it is easy to deduce an ethical positioning for either the author or the character.

The first of these ways by which America can be felt is through language. Clearly, as a writer Steinbeck makes artistic choices with language. Is this the best word to convey that meaning to the audience? This we all do, in written or oral expression. But can there be an ethics of language, or are all words necessarily neutral? If words, however, are used to convey meaning toward an audience, then they also bear intentionality. Speech is a willful action in community that may bear good or harmful effects.

Steinbeck draws our attention to language several times in *Charley*: "One of my purposes was to listen, to hear speech, speech rhythms, overtones and emphasis. For speech is so much more than words and sentences" (95–96). Steinbeck's fear is a national packaging of speech, so that we begin to lose our speech identity as regionalism and localism. Instead, we all sound like televisions. In addition to losing this identity, moreover, one loses a sense of communication with audience. The itinerant actor whom he meets observes, "You know when show people come into what they call the sticks, they have a contempt for the yokels. It took me a little time, but when I learned that there aren't any yokels I began to get on fine. I learned respect for my audience" (134). Speech, or writing, bears a two-way ethical pattern: selecting the right words to best convey the message and honoring the audience with understanding and respect.

If this is the ideal, language also has a darker underbelly. It can be used to hurt, maim, and destroy the hearer. This arises of course in the infamous cheerleaders scene, where southern women hurled racial slurs at African-American schoolchildren. What troubles Steinbeck in particular, in addition to the general oppressive atmosphere of hate and cruelty, is the deliberateness of the language:

> But now I heard the words, bestial and filthy and degenerate. In a long and unprotected life I have seen and heard the vomitings of demoniac humans before. Why then did these screams fill me with a shocked and sickened sorrow?
>
> The words written down are dirty, carefully and selectedly filthy. But there was something far worse here than dirt, a kind of frightening witches' Sabbath. Here was no spontaneous cry of anger, of insane rage. (227–28)

This is deliberate vilification of human life through language, and Steinbeck makes clear that it is ethically wrong.

As a counterpart, in a sense, Steinbeck's writing everywhere in the travel-journal is deliberate and keenly crafted. Nearly every page turns up descriptive passages so exquisite one wants to read them several times. At certain points the descriptive prose echoes the clear, precise passages of *The Log from the Sea of Cortez*. From the Mojave Desert Steinbeck writes,

> The beaten earth appears defeated and dead, but it only appears so. A vast and inventive organization of living matter survives by seeming to have lost. The gray and dusty sage wears oily armor to protect its inward small moistness. Some plants engorge themselves with water in the rare rainfall and store it for future use. Animal life wears a hard, dry skin or an outer skeleton to defy the desiccation. (191)

From the Badlands of North Dakota he writes,

> It was so beautiful that I stopped near a thicket of dwarfed and wind-warped cedars and junipers, and once stopped I was caught, trapped in color and dazzled by the clarity of the light. Against the descending sun the battlements were dark and clean-lined, while to the east, where the uninhibited light poured slantwise, the strange landscape shouted with color. And the night, far from being frightful, was lovely beyond thought, for the stars were close, and although there was no moon, the starlight made a silver glow in the sky. (141)

Even the traffic gets its descriptive due:

> First the traffic struck me like a tidal wave and carried me along, a bit of shiny flotsam bounded in front by a gasoline truck half a block long. Behind me was an enormous cement mixer on wheels, its big howitzer revolving as it proceeded. (116)

Such passages, and there are many more, merit our attention for in themselves they provide the lie to the Cheerleaders' vitriol. There is immense and exquisite beauty in language. And it serves an ethical, as well as aesthetic, good when it brings beauty and delight to the reader.

The second major area of ethical inquiry in *Charley* involves the nature of people. The issue might appear superficial. After all, Steinbeck inevitably met many people on his journey. Most of them he liked. The ones who were reticent or taciturn he generally poked gentle fun at. The ones who were bigoted or mean-spirited, he generally destroyed under Rocinante's wheels and his sharp disdain. But at each level he wonders *who are these people of the nation?* What typifies them? At one point he reflects on words from a friend:

> There used to be a thing or a commodity we put great store by. It was called the People. Find out where the People have gone. Maybe they never existed, but if there ever were the People, that's the commodity the Declaration was talking about, and Mr. Lincoln. Come to think of it, I've known a few, but not many. Wouldn't it be silly if the Constitution had been talking about a young man whose life centers around a whistle, a wink, and a Wildroot? (151–52)

Clearly the words evoke the sentiments of Ma Joad in *The Grapes of Wrath*, but what do they signify now?

By and large Steinbeck functions as a journalist of the people he meets. He reports objectively. He dramatizes them in a situation so that we see them as if on a stage and are therefore left to draw our own conclusions. And he builds his stage as expansively as he can. We meet characters who share a fairly nondescript, fleeting moment there to complicated human dramas. But we do not merely survey those dramas. Steinbeck positions them in such a way, with varying conflicts of character, that the reader draws abrupt conclusions not only about the nature of people, but also about where they go right and where they go wrong.

One way we see this is through frequent comparisons, as with the two veterinarians who treat Charley. Steinbeck had written earlier, "In establishing contact with strange people, Charley is my ambassador" (59). He is an intermediary, a linkage, a gauge. How he reacts to people, and how they react to him, reveals much to Steinbeck about their personhood. So it is that the first vet, long settled into an alcoholic discontent, looks upon Charley as a thing: "He raised Charley's lip with a shaking hand, then turned up an eyelid and let it fall back" (159). After some meaningless blather, the vet gives his diagnosis: "Probably a cold." When Steinbeck pushes him for a closer diagnosis, he meets with this vagary: "Look here. He's an old dog. Old dogs get aches and pains. That's just the way it is" (160). After he pays the bill, an exercise in futility, Steinbeck reflects: "It wasn't that this veterinary didn't like animals. I think he didn't like himself, and when that is so the subject usually must find an area for dislike outside himself. Else he would have to admit his self-contempt" (160). Such people, essentially disliking themselves, transfer that dislike on others. A careful reader can follow that pattern in any number of characters from Steinbeck's novels and short stories.

Charley did not have a cold, of course. He had prostatitis, and he still needed treatment. Remembering "the poor incompetent veterinary" and "how Charley had looked at him with pained wonder and contempt," Steinbeck sought additional help for his comrade. In Amarillo he had a veterinarian come to his hotel to make another try at diagnosis. But this vet didn't undertake it with a quick glance and glib diagnosis. Instead he reached out to Charley and connected with him: "Then the young vet's hands went down and moved over hips and distended abdomen—trained and knowing hands. Charley sighed a great sigh and his tail wagged up slowly from the floor and down again. Charley put himself in the man's care, completely confident" (207). An astute reader might even hear echoes in the prose from the concluding paragraph of *The Grapes of Wrath*, where Rose of Sharon breastfeeds the starving man. Here by a healing touch, the vet achieves an accurate diagnosis.

The play between the two veterinarians is not unusual in the dialectics of people groups that Steinbeck plays on in the book. But this is the nature of the American people that he covers. Some are flawed, some deeply so, and some drink deep of that milk of human kindness. Save for the cheerleaders scene, and the prejudiced hitchhiker, both of whom he denounces in no uncertain terms, Steinbeck maintains the literary guise of objective reporter, recording the experience and letting us, the readers, draw our own conclusions.

But the "guise" of a reporter is really just that—a guise. No matter how objective the journalist, or the travel-journalist in this case, attempts to be, he or she is making judgments. Nor can Steinbeck escape this. Such judgments are made in any number of ways. For example, context is always revealing. Steinbeck tells us that the first veterinarian was perhaps hung over. That neither excuses nor stipulates his incompetence. It may be a companion, a context, for his incompetence, perhaps. As such Steinbeck draws a negative picture of him that *heightens* his essential wrong.

Similarly the journalist frames attitudes, as we saw earlier, by language. Even with his brilliant ear for the rhythms and moods of human speech, Steinbeck subtly stages those rhythms and moods to carry emotional weight. In the poignant scene of Robbie the would-be hairdresser, actually one of the longer stage scenes in the book, we first meet him and his father as a sullen pair—emotional mirrors of each other really, even if for varied reasons. Consequently, their character and their speech are sharp and acerbic. Like the two veterinarians, Steinbeck has a choice of two ways to go: to give his diagnosis and go to sleep, or to try to touch the situation and ameliorate the condition. Mostly he listens, but also asks questions, like the second vet: probing fingers. Only when they laugh does the tension leave the room. As Papa says, "Now that we got our hackles down, what do you think of this hair-dressing beautician stuff?" (156).

In *Travels with Charley* Steinbeck works by implication, letting contexts, language, and staging take the place of overt moral judgments. Yet, the judgments are there; the values clear. How we act, toward ourselves and others, with patience, consideration, and understanding are ethical goods. How we act, toward ourselves and others, by using them as things, by despising life, and by suppressing ambitions are ethical wrongs. The full scope of his sense of ethical virtue was developing, guided slowly but surely in his complete absorption in the *Morte D'Arthur*.

6

A Knight's Tale

In *The Canterbury Tales* Chaucer's Knight is a nonpareil, a paragon of courtly virtue and justice. In Chaucer's memorable telling, the Knight represents both political order and also a divine order as ordained by the stars. Because of his prominence and high order, "The Knight's Tale" leads all the others. His is the lodestar by which we judge the rectitude, the frivolity, and the downright foolishness of all who follow. The hilarity of the Wife of Bath acquires an edge when compared to the stately conduct of the Knight. Ironically, Alice's story is set "In th' olde dayes of the Kyng Arthour." But it is neither myth nor fairy tale. For Alice it is a playground for her romp on the "sovereynetee" of women. In the same way, the Miller's bawdy fabliau can be measured against the Knight's stately decorum—and found wanting.

What, however, gives the Knight such status? It is not simply nobility in breeding, a proximity to the court, nor, for that matter, shiny armor and a good horse. Instead, it's a code of conduct, a way of living. This is the code of chivalry. We first meet the Knight in the preface like this:

> A Knyght ther was, and that a worthy man,
> That fro the tyme that he first bigan
> To riden out, he loved chivalrie,
> Trouth and honour, fredom and curteisie.

Thereby Chaucer establishes the four ethical virtues of knighthood. The Knight loved chivalry. Chivalry was his calling, part of his vows and station. But for the Knight this is not mere obligation; he loved it. How do we understand *love*? Not as adored, for that would be infatuation. Nor as enchanted, for that would be some self-centered emotion, and the Knight was called to be selfless. Closer to the mark of Chaucer's meaning would be to say he was wholly and passionately committed to it.

Then Chaucer defines the constituent qualities of this chivalry. *Trouthe,* derived from the Old English *troth,* is fidelity and loyalty. This would be first of all to his vows, second to his sovereign. The second quality is *honour,* which means honorable deeds. Negatively this suggests the avoidance of petty quarrels and squabbles, but more specifically it means those deeds that uphold justice. *Fredom* is a more elusive virtue in its meaning. It's a spirit, a way of living that is magnanimous, noble, and generous. Even this bears qualification, for it is far more than merely a dispensation of alms to the needy, although it involves that too. It is a fatherly attitude toward others, akin to the king or nobleman who stands in judgment and grants a "boon" or verdict. It signifies a deep and calm wisdom. The last, *curteisie,* is the exercise of courtly manners, in accord with the Knight's elevated social status. Chaucer further defines it as "curteis he was, lowely, and servysable." The ideal Knight is modest (*lowely*), and ready to serve.

For Chaucer these are more than job descriptions. They are ethical virtues by which we can measure the rights or wrongs of all the other pilgrims. But more than that they signify a divine order acted through Christ's representatives on earth. All this also is the frame for "The Knight's Tale," a careful study of divine order and human affairs. Chaucer bears mention here as a foreword to Steinbeck's work on Malory because many of the same ethical virtues inform *Morte D'Arthur*, but Malory's is a tale of the steady darkening of the human spirit and the slow drift away from these lodestars of right behavior. Steinbeck may have been attracted to the sheer adventure of the stories; he surely couldn't escape awareness of the clangors of ethical conflict.

A Boy and His Book

Steinbeck's lifelong love affair with Malory is itself a well-known story. He provides a full rendition in the introduction to *The Acts of King Arthur and his Noble Knights*: "One day, an aunt gave me a book.... I stared at the black print with hatred, and then, gradually, the pages opened and let me in. The magic happened" (1).[1] It was the adventure, the magic, the sheer transport of the language that "let him in." This he wanted to share with the modern reader: "I wanted to set them down in plain present-day speech... to set the stories down in meaning as they were written, leaving out nothing and adding nothing" (3).

Influences of *Morte* may be seen in several of Steinbeck's works. The Grail Quest is notable in *Cup of Gold*. The concept of the Round Table and rather ignoble knights colors all of *Tortilla*

---

[1] In *The True Adventures of John Steinbeck, Writer* (New York: Viking, 1984), Jackson Benson describes the youthful influence of Malory on Steinbeck and his sister:

> John and his younger sister, Mary, would read the Arthur tales together and then recreate them in play, going into the fields with lath swords, cardboard helmets, and the pony, Jill, to search for the Grail. Mary and John had established a special relationship. While she was assigned the role of squire, she more often acted the part of Sancho Panza. When her brother was young, she got most of his jobs for him. She tried to steer him away from trouble, and when trouble came, she tried to moderate the consequences.

Flat.[2] *Sweet Thursday* completes the Cannery Row Cycle with Arthurian elements. But during the 1950s, with his growing despondency over the state of American moral qualities, Steinbeck pursued an ethical salvation in Malory with greedy avidity. To study the Winchester manuscripts he and Elaine lived abroad for long periods of time.[3] Eugene Vinaver, who had just published the three-volume edition of Malory's works, grew in stature to be everything Steinbeck idealized for himself. As Camelot hovered above him like a cynosure, Steinbeck's vision of America seemed to turn proportionately darker.

---

[2] In *The Wide World of John Steinbeck* Peter Lisca points out dissimilarities between the two works (New Brunswick: Rutgers University Press, 1958). On the other hand, Arthur F. Kinney, in "The Arthurian Cycle in *Tortilla Flat*," *Modern Fiction Studies* 11.1 (Spring 1965): 11–20, discusses the many similarities. Steinbeck himself acknowledged the similarities in a 1934 letter to Mavis McIntosh:

> The book has a very definite theme. I thought it was clear enough. I have expected that the plan of the Arthurian cycle would be recognized, that my Garvaine and Launcelot, my Arthur and Galahad would be recognized. Even the incident of the Sangreal in the search of the forest is not clear enough I guess. The form is that of the Malory version, the coming of Arthur and the mystic quality of owning a house, the forming of the round table, the adventures of the knights and finally, the mystic translation of Danny (*LL*, 96–97).

For a study of Steinbeck's aims and difficulties in composition of *Morte*, see Michael Sundermeier, "Why Steinbeck Didn't Finish His *Arthur—The Acts of King Arthur and His Noble Knights* (1976)," *Steinbeck's Posthumous Work: Essays in Criticism*, ed. Tetsumaro Hayashi and Thomas J. Moore, Steinbeck Monograph Series no. 14, (1989): 34–42.

[3] For background on Steinbeck's research and writing, see Roy S. Simmonds, "The Unrealized Dream: Steinbeck's Modern Version of Malory," *Steinbeck and the Arthurian Theme*, ed. Tetsumaro Hayashi, Steinbeck Monograph Series, no. 5 (1975).

Steinbeck's attitude is well summarized in his letters of the time, several of which are cited in chapter 4. The sentiments toll through many passages like drumbeats in a funeral march. Perhaps, in this psychological climate, Camelot was an escape. A skeptic might observe that during the years of working on Malory, Steinbeck did a lot of work without doing much of anything. The final production, published posthumously, is but a scant portion of the original. Steinbeck took a sabbatical from America and entered a Sabbath rest. He took a leave of absence and just left. After all, he had done enough and was wealthy enough that he earned the right to a harmless hobby in his dotage, or so the skeptics would have it.

Steinbeck saw it differently. It is true that when he worked deliberately and methodically he tended to produce some of his best work. *The Grapes of Wrath, East of Eden,* and the short stories of the 1930s stand as testimony. When he rushed recklessly with a manuscript, as with *The Winter of Our Discontent* or the lamentable *Burning Bright,* his artistry suffered. The story of Camelot, to his mind, was to be of the former sort, whatever the deficiencies of the final, unfinished product. He worked deliberately, for he was looking both inside himself and outward toward his age. He sought nothing less than an ethical bulwark to erect against both, to redirect the course of both. In his introduction Steinbeck observed,

> In that scene were all the vices that ever were—and courage and sadness and frustration, but particularly gallantry—perhaps the only single quality of man that the West has invented. I think my sense of right and wrong, my feeling of *noblesse oblige,* and any thought I may have against the oppressor and for the oppressed, came from this secret book. It did not outrage my sensibilities as nearly all the children's books did. It did not seem strange to me that Uther Pendragon wanted the wife of his vassal and took her by trickery. I was not frightened to find that there were evil knights, as well as

> noble ones. In my town there were men who wore the clothes of virtue whom I knew to be bad. In pain or sorrow or confusion, I went back to my magic book. If I could not choose my way at the crossroads of love and loyalty, neither could Lancelot. I could understand the darkness of Mordred because he was in me too; and there was some Galahad in me, but perhaps not enough. The Grail feeling was there, however, deep-planted, and perhaps always will be. (2)

The Grail feeling—the sense that some ideals are worth pursing no matter how veiled, nor how difficult the pursuit—was his ultimate aim.

If Steinbeck identified closely with his project, seeing both himself and America in it, it may be because he believed Malory did so with his own work. Jackson Benson quotes from a letter written to Elizabeth Otis:

> Malory has been studied as a translator, as a soldier, as a rebel, as a religious, as an expert in courtesy, as nearly everything you can think of except one, and that is what he was—a novelist. The Morte is the first and one of the greatest of novels in the English language. And only a novelist could think of it. A novelist not only puts down a story but he is the story. He is each one of the characters in a greater or a less degree. And because he is usually a moral man in intention and honest in his approach, he sets things down as truly as he can.

A novel may be said to be the man who writes it. Now it is nearly always true that a novelist, perhaps unconsciously, identifies himself with one chief or central character in his novel. Into this character he puts not only what he thinks he is but what he hopes to be. We can call this spokesman the self-character. You will find one in every one of my books and in the novels of everyone I can remember.... I supposed my own symbol character has my dream wish of wisdom and acceptance.

Now it seems to me that Malory's self-character would be Launcelot. All of the perfections he knew went into this character, all of the things of which he thought himself capable. But, being an honest man he found faults in himself, faults of vanity, faults of violence, faults even of disloyalty and these would naturally find their way into his dream character....[4]

Steinbeck extended his argument of the writer being both the book and the "self-character" to the Grail Quest itself. Here too the writer explores his own depravities as he engages a quest for moral certitude. It was not at all unusual for Steinbeck to write in such a way, usually in a journal or notebook, on his ideas for and progress with the work he was writing. However eagerly Steinbeck engaged the project, and however important he saw it as a redemptive moral creed, the work, however, did not proceed smoothly.

Part of the difficulty lay in Steinbeck's differing perceptions of his work compared with the original. The question of Camelot is an intriguing one, for even with the years of study, researching, and translating *Morte*, Steinbeck seems misguided by its central thematic and historical issues. What he did perceive is clear: an heroic but failed effort to stave off the tidal wave of disorder, an inherent nobility that enables a man to rise above his dangerous adversaries, and a deeply compelling adventure story. In his February 25, 1964, letter to Jacqueline Kennedy, Steinbeck wrote:

> The 15th century and our own have so much in common—loss of authority, loss of gods, loss of heroes, and loss of lovely pride. When such a hopeless muddled need occurs, it does seem to me that the hungry hearts of men distill their best and truest essence, and that essence becomes man, and that man a hero so that all men can be reassured that such things are

---

[4] Jackson J. Benson, *John Steinbeck, Writer* (New York: Viking Press, 19984) 810–11.

possible. The fact that all of these words—hero, myth, pride, even victory, have been muddied and sicklied by the confusion and pessimism of the times only described the times. (*LL*, 793)

A few days later he added, "I do believe that strength and purity tie almost exclusively in the struggle—the becoming" (795).

Several elements there strike one as contradictory. If strength and purity lie in the struggle, we simply have a Sisyphean cycle with no *telos*. If we have a loss of authority, then what exactly is the authority we have lost? Loss of gods—but exactly what myths does he reference? And what constitutes heroism, or in what may we take pride, for that matter? Steinbeck has eschewed reason for slogans. All of these ideals, as he observed to Mrs. Kennedy, "have been muddied and sicklied by the confusion and pessimism of the times."

In spite of his immersion in Malory, and surely such Arthurian predecessors as Bede, William of Malmesbury, Geoffrey of Monmouth, Wace, and Layamon, Steinbeck misses or disregards several of the essential thematic and ethical issues of these works. Why was this? Three factors emerge. First, while the Arthurian legend in all of its manifestations, at least up through Tennyson's *Idylls*, was perceived as a deeply religious work, Steinbeck perceived it primarily as political. Order for him was not something derived from or imposed by any supreme authority, but something emanating from orderly interaction of humans themselves. Second, while christological evidence is primary in the legends, and accepted as a *de facto* reality, Steinbeck perceived the story of Christ on a par with any myth.[5] Finally, Malory's principal concern, largely working

[5] One of Steinbeck's most direct testaments of rejection occurs in a March 30, 1959, letter to Elizabeth Otis:

as he was from the French *Queste* and the *Alliterative Morte Arthure*, was to understand the massively complicated figure of Lancelot and the conundrum of love, chivalry, and betrayal. This pattern of the romance, perhaps, formed the primary appeal to Steinbeck's moralistic sensibilities. To set these distinctions concretely, it is helpful to view the moral, social, and political disintegration that Steinbeck asserts in *America* against the very different perceptions of Malory.

In *America and Americans*, Steinbeck concludes in broad strokes that our moral decay originates in our obsession for things, our failure to conserve natural resources, the dominance of the Corporate Man, and our failures in child-rearing, among others. These failures are all self-inflicted and self-perpetuating. Therefore, the corrective arises from a reversal of the primary conditions of our moral collapse by an assertion of human will. Perhaps his own best summary of the ethic appears in Steinbeck's February 28, 1964, letter to Jacqueline Kennedy: "Probably the greatness of our country resides in the fact that we have not made it and are still trying. No–I do believe that strength and purity lie almost exclusively in the struggle–the becoming" (*LL*, 795).

Malory's vision differed, and was certainly less existential than Steinbeck's. From its origins, and retained by Malory, the Arthurian legend finds its basis in the concept of *Logres*. Camelot institutes the city of God and has divine sanction. Chapters 5–8 of *Morte* detail the Archbishop of Canterbury

---

Yesterday, Easter, we went to services in the Bruton church. I found it nostalgically moving because I knew it all from my childhood, but also I found again that there is nothing in it that I need or want. Elaine both needs and wants it and so she may have it. But I'll take my birds any day and the processional of the sun. (LL 623

overseeing Arthur's withdrawal of the sword and his coronation at the Feast of Pentecost. A religious figure—not a political one—bestows the honor. The action occurs over the course of the High Holy Days. The sword is withdrawn at Christmas, signifying a divine incarnation in human form. In this case it is Arthur, and the sword is his symbol to order the Round Table, the efficacious agent of his will. Obviously the twelve knights resemble the twelve disciples. At New Year's Day the jousts are celebrated, and from these the first Arthurian knights are selected. At Candlemas (a February 2 feast for the Virgin Mary) Arthur removes the sword yet again before the high lords of Britain. They acclaim him king, but the archbishop delays until Pentecost, the day of empowerment by the Holy Spirit.

Here, as in earlier versions, the coronation is depicted as a powerful religious service. The alliterative *Morte Arthure* (c. 1360), with which both Malory and Steinbeck were familiar, describes Arthur thus:

> Than knelis the crownede kynge and kryes levede:
> "I thanke thee, Gode, of thy grace, with a gud wylle,
> That gafe us vertue and witt to vencows this beryns
> And us has grauntede the gree of theis gret lords."[6]

The *Logres* incarnates the word of God in the political order of the human kingdom. Both the internal and external evidence of Malory's *Morte* provide the sense that Camelot is a spiritual entity, ordered to enact God's will and justice on earth.

Meanwhile, Steinbeck continued to labor hard over his telling into the 1960s. Elaine reported her husband working for

---

[6] Anonymous, *Morte Arthure, Middle English Literature*, ed. Charles W. Dunn and Edward T. Byrnes (New York: Harcourt Brace Jovanovich, 1973) 268.

two to three hours "before coming up for a cup of coffee." But that work was also interrupted by trips to *Morte* locales, dozens of trips to bookshops in hope of finding an important bit of information, and plenty of time spent with visitors. Jackson Benson commented that he also felt "at times, overwhelmed by detail: he had to make decision after decision while taking into consideration a dozen factors simultaneously—tone, sound, image, emphasis, perspective, narrative coherence, character development and consistency, and theme" (847). His greatest difficulty, however, lay in disagreements with Elizabeth Otis. She had been pushing him from the start to write a novel, not a retelling. For her the version she reviewed was fragmented and lifeless. She wanted another *Once and Future King*.

For all his labor, part of the reason lay in the task that Steinbeck set for himself. The original fifteenth-century English is an overwhelmingly rich language, both lyrical and profound, like a thunderstorm clearing its throat. In Malory's hands, the language matches the action at every step; its greatness lies in the resonance of tone and style as much as story.[7] To be sure, Steinbeck has his own richness of language; "When Uther and Merlin and Sir Ulfius rode through the starlit darkness towards the sea, the fog moved restlessly over the moors like wispy ghosts inflating clothes" (10). As Steinbeck himself observed, "There are such profundities in Malory sometimes hidden in a phrase, I have to be very careful not to miss them and

[7] Several translations and retellings of *Morte* exist today. I prefer R. M. Lumiansky's version (New York: Macmillan, 1982) as the most readable and clear, and which is used here. Furthermore, Lumiansky conflates both the Caxton edition (1498 and 1529) and the Winchester, discovered in 1934. Quotations will be cited parenthetically as *Morte* and the page number The manuscripts differ, but the comparison turns up many flaws in each (the primitive printing presses spawned them at an enormous rate). These Lumiansky resolves them in an authoritative and complete volume.

sometimes blow them up a little to make them apparent" (Benson, 847–48). While Tennyson achieved greatness in *The Idylls of the King* by the sheer power of his poetic rhythms, and while T. H. White achieved greatness by the power of story, it seems that Steinbeck was indecisive on the one hand by his intrigue with language and, on the other, by Otis's pressure to write a popular novel.

In any event, Otis's challenging letter to Steinbeck was met with dismay as he had, once again, to defend his project. Part of that defense includes this passage:

> I am not writing this to titillate the ear of the twentieth century. Perhaps I am overambitious, but I am trying to make it available, not desirable. I want the remote feeling of the myth, not the intimate feeling of today's man who in his daily thought may change tomorrow but who in his deeper perceptions, I am convinced, does not change at all. In a word I have not been trying to write a popular book but a permanent book. (Benson, 850)

From the point of view of our study, however, the problems lay at a deeper and more profound level.

Ethical Malady

In Steinbeck's perception of the ethical world of *Le Morte,* the highest virtue is honor. This ranges from personal adherence to vows to upholding community values. In his chapter on Morgan Le Fay, Steinbeck sets up a dialectic between Arthur and his half-sister. Steinbeck describes her as "a dark, handsome, passionate woman, and cruel and ambitious" (119). Trained in the dark arts, she carefully plotted Arthur's murder. Her motivation was to increase her own power by destruction of what is good and orderly. Steinbeck must have loved her as a villain, for she incarnated all those evil passions that he saw infesting his own culture. So too she represents the framework for ethical wrong in the story. When individuals set self over the common good, when they seek power over obedience, they are villains.

But we have to consider Morgan's case beyond Steinbeck's practical interest to an ethical interest. Bernard Gert insists that choosing evil is an irrational choice:

> All rational persons desire to avoid evils; they need have no particular concern about yellow. Defining an evil as the object of an irrational desire provides an objective account of evil, and yet not one which is independent of rational people. The definition makes it clear that a rational person seeks to avoid evils for himself, it does not require that he be concerned with avoiding evils for others.[8]

Evil then is the object of irrational desire. "Rational persons," argues Gert, "not only cannot desire evil, they must also desire to avoid it."[9] While Gert's argument leaves substantial room for debate, it does bear interesting implications for how we, and presumably Steinbeck, see Morgan. First, rational desires, we assume, are those in accord with standards of commonweal. It is wrong to injure others because it curtails their right to an orderly and peaceful life. Furthermore, this valuing of order may require one to set aside personal desires. This is precisely the requirement of the Round Table when the knights take vows of self-sacrificial loyalty. The second point that we can see comporting with Steinbeck's ethics at the time is that irrational desires are destructive. We witness this with Morgan when she switches Arthur's sword and connives to get him to fight against his own sword Excalibur with an inferior weapon. Arthur is wounded and discovers that the knights around him have been

---

[8] Bernard Gert, *Morality: Its Nature and Justification* (New York: Oxford University Press, 1998) 49.

[9] Ibid.

woven into illusions by a net of Morgan's necromancy. Even more disruptive, Arthur admits, is the personal pain the treachery caused him, for "I have honored Morgan Le Fay, my sister, given in to her, and loved her better than my other kin" (128).

If the distinction between rational and irrational desires, orderly and disruptive of order, creates an ethical framework for Steinbeck's Arthurian world, it is nonetheless very different from Malory's. For in Malory's world an entire cosmology is upheld or threatened. Malory's cosmology is essentially Ptolemaic, but clearly, as we have already seen, overlaid with the broad expanse of Christian belief. This view informs every deed of every knight. They do not simply act on their own; they act within some grand, sweeping plan. Steinbeck's retelling dutifully retains Malory's references to God, but missing is this broad interconnectivity, where each human action occurs within some divine scheme.

In many ways medieval cosmology was adapted from Greek cosmology, particularly Plato's representative *Timaeus*, his "discourse on the nature of the universe." Socrates' argument presupposes a "first cause" that is eternal, necessarily so since the universe is temporal and subject to change. Therefore it had to have a cause that was unchanging. Furthermore, Timaeus argues that their first cause is good. This we discover in the order of the universe, and the audience accepts that order is always good while disorder is always bad.[10] By various steps, a full review of which is not necessary to our study here, Plato demonstrated that the Prime Mover created order out of chaos. Therefore the eternal Prime Mover necessarily stands outside of that temporal order he has made. But he went one step further, for in humans he put intelligence

---

[10] This concept, of course, is the very basis for Plato's *Republic*. The state mirrors divine and universal order.

in soul and soul in body. Thereby he formed an indelible link between himself, who is all soul, and the temporal order. Intelligence in soul is our guide (although not stated overtly in the *Timaeus*) to actions that accord with the divine order and harmony.

The cosmology inherited from the Greeks situated Earth at the center of the universe. Above it revolved, in a clockwise motion, the seven heavenly bodies. These were, in order from the earth: Moon, Mercury, Venus, Sun, Mars, Jupiter, and Saturn. Above these, moving in a counterclockwise direction, was the body of fixed stars. But two figures outside an essentially closed system were involved within it. The first of these of course was the all-necessary Prime Mover, who established the whole and the natural laws that keep it running. The other is Dame Fortune, or Fate, whose spindle roots in earth but she herself resides outside the system. At her spindle of necessity she can exercise considerable influence over human affairs, yet she remains unconcerned about those affairs. She is kept company by her three daughters. Lachesis is the daughter of things past, who controls inner and outer spheres of the fixed stars. Clotho is the daughter of things present, who controls the outer spheres. Atropos is the daughter of things future, who controls the inner spheres.

By the time this fundamental cosmology carried into medieval England, and the importance of this will be seen momentarily, the rise of the church had thoroughly Christianized it. The framework remains essentially the same, but the concentric circles now lay within a rectangle representing the whole of all things on heaven and earth.[11] Stationed at the four corners are the mighty powers of the four

---

[11] The best pictorial representation of the "Ptolemaic" universe derives from Hartmann Schedel's *Liber Chronicarum*, or the "Nuremburg Chronicle" of 1493.

winds. They may be seen as similar to Fortune, but the difference is that they are directed by God. Within a large circle resides God on his throne, surrounded by his choristers, who also, in turn, surround the spheres. God is above all things, but also holds in control and is involved in all things. Interestingly, the medieval cosmology retains the Prime Mover, but it is placed as the outermost concentric circle.

This cosmology, held by Malory, creates a holistic world and life view in the *Morte*, one not shared by Steinbeck. But this cosmology also caused Malory his greatest ethical difficulty, and this is the essential issue that I believe either escaped Steinbeck or that he simply ignored. Moreover, the ethics of communal belief and committed action is absolutely essential to the whole legendary material that Steinbeck worked with in his translation. For Malory, the supreme paradox was this: how could Lancelot, most gallant of the knights, pervert his gallantry in his sin with Guinevere? While the French *Queste* condemns the sin and requires penance of Lancelot, Malory persists in describing Lancelot's intentional virtue. To the end, Malory insists that Lancelot was "the best of any synfull man of the worlde" (863). Malory thereby relativizes both the sin of Lancelot and the ethics of chivalry to something like "doing the best you can." Indeed, Lancelot supplants any spiritual goal with this one earthly and relative goal:

> And all my grete dedis of armys that I have done for the moste party was all for the quenys sake, and for hir sake wolde I do batayle *were hit ryght other wronge*. And never dud I batayle all only for Goddis sake, but for to wynne worship and to cause me the bettir to be beloved, and litill or nought I thanked never God of hit. [emphasis mine] (897)

What Malory attempts to forge is a bifurcated ethic. When done in the name of Camelot, Lancelot's mighty deeds are blameless. When done self-interestedly, they are blameworthy.

But neither Lancelot nor Malory can have it so. The affair with Guinevere is simply wrong, and, as Lancelot confesses, it occurred because he transferred loyalty from God to the queen. Consequently, *Logres* shatters. Humanity now lies, as Steinbeck recognized, east of Eden.

There are no roadmaps back. In spite of Lancelot's valiant but self-maddening redemptive effort to find the grail, he is not permitted. Nor can he accept that he can't. The crack in Camelot widens and neither Lancelot nor all the king's men can ever put Camelot together again.

Steinbeck's World

Steinbeck's Arthurian world is one of illustrious events, dutifully reported in high style, yet it clearly is not the world shot through with a divine ethical "ought," or duties and obligations, that Malory worked under. This contrast may be seen in several ways: the coming of Arthur, the *Logres,* the calling of the *comitatus,* the nature of Merlin, and the nature of evil.

Steinbeck follows the opening passages of Malory fairly closely. His great effort here was reductive, eliding certain passages to arrive at a smooth story. As part of that reductionism, he cut certain matters that were essential to Malory's world, particularly the high sacerdotalism of Arthur's calling. For Malory, Arthur was appointed king by divine decree, and his calling to that position had to be witnessed by miraculous signs. The fulfillment of the divine decree was to maintain justice and order on earth.

With Arthur sick and his enemies encroaching on his kingdom, Merlin intervened with the highest earthly spiritual source, the Archbishop of Canterbury, entreating him to gather the lords and landholders in London. The appointed date: Christmas, for "Jesus, who was born on that night, would in

His great mercy show some miracle; since He had come to be King of mankind, he would show by some miracle who should rightly be king of this realm" (*Morte*, 7). We notice the connection between the kingship of Jesus and the human king. From the outset they are intertwined. A second element derives from the ceremony: "All this was ordained to keep the lords and the commons together, for the Archbishop trusted that God would make known who should win the sword" (8). The ceremony was designed to promote order and harmony among all levels of society—instilling the justice of God and the order of the heavenly spheres into human affairs.

Curious twists of action follow. First, when Arthur's stepbrother Sir Kay loses his sword in the jousts, Arthur spots the sword in the stone, easily lifts it out, and delivers it to Sir Kay. Examining Arthur on how he got the sword, Sir Ector, his foster father, recognizes the unofficial kingship of Arthur. He responds, "'Sire,' said Sir Ector, 'because God will have it so; for never could a man have drawn out this sword but he who shall be rightful king of this land. Now let me see whether ye can put the sword back as it was and pull it out again'" (9). Ector recognizes God's will in the act. Arthur pulls it out a second time. At Twelfth Day Arthur pulls it out again, while all others fail. So too on Candelmass. So too at Pentecost. Finally all recognize Arthur as king:

> Therewith they kneeled at once, both rich and poor, and cried Arthur mercy because they had delayed him so long. But Arthur forgave them, took the sword between both his hands, and offered upon the altar where the Archbishop was; so he was made a knight by the best man who was there. Soon the coronation was arranged, and there he was sworn unto his lords and his commons to be a true king, to stand with true justice thenceforth during the days of his life. (11)

Interesting qualities emerge in those lines. First, Arthur lays the sword before the archbishop. His reign will be in service to God. Second, the aim of his rule is to promote true justice. He will labor to establish the kingdom of God on this earth—the *Logres*.

The concept of *Logres*, the kingdom of God on earth, is predicated upon the Gospel of John, where Jesus is described as the *Logos*, the word of God made incarnate. John asserts three conditions of the *Logos*: "In the beginning was the Word, and the Word was with God, and the Word was God. He was with God in the beginning" (John 1:1) The first quality is the eternality of the word. He was there at the beginning; therefore, he always has been. Second, the *Logos* is an individual being, marked by his own nature, who was *with* God from the beginning. One cannot be with another unless that one is other than the person whom he stands in relation with. But, third, the *Logos* is himself God, wholly divine and sharing all the attributes of God. Philosophically, we may distinguish between attributes and functions. It was the task of this *Logos*, as John argues for the rest of his Gospel, to bring light to the darkness and to do so as God incarnate in human form. His function was to establish the kingdom of God on earth. *Logres* is that kingdom in which the king (Arthur) stands in the stead and as representative of the *Logos*. Arthur does not so much ascend to the throne as he is ordained to the throne. This sacred task the archbishop fulfills. He is sworn to "serve with true justice." As his knights are in vassalage to Arthur, so is he in vassalage to the *Logos*.

To exact true justice, the king must identify and root out evil in his kingdom. For this he requires a *comitatus*, a body of knights in sworn service to him to enact true justice. These constitute the Round Table of Arthur. And here also lay the tragedy of the *Morte*, for these knights were to be emblematic of the court, which was itself emblematic of the divine order. As God ordered the circles of the universe, so his representative on earth rules the connectivity of the Round Table. The knights that joined that circle were expected, like Chaucer's Knyght, to be paragons of virtue, riding forth from the table to enact good deeds, to bring light to the darkness. But indeed, they are human, all too human. While several of the knights truly fulfill their role, too many supplant the ideal with personal desire. Lancelot, a profound psychological study, would do good, but does bad. In spite of his mighty acts of arms, he is a monstrous landscape of personal urges and uncontrollable desires. And Arthur himself has failings, most notably in his last battle at Cornwall, which he rushes into without his usual preparations and against his leaders' advice. William Matthews observes, "Despite his belated longing for a savior's role, Arthur is still not free from the tragic coil of his own making."[12] If the *comitatus* represents God's rule on earth, it is through deeply flawed means.

Although Steinbeck relates an abbreviated and objective accounting of these events, his rendition lacks entirely the backdrop of Malory's world and life view. But it is with the last two items in particular—the role of Merlin and the workings of good and evil—that his ethical stance differs most widely from Malory.

In Steinbeck's telling Merlin is a man of mystery.

> Now Merlin was a wise and subtle man with strange and secret powers of prophecy and those deceptions of the ordinary and the obvious which are called magic. Merlin knew the winding channels of the human mind, and also he was

---

[12] William Matthews, "Sin and Punishment in the Alliterative *Morte Arthur*," *Arthur King of Britain*, ed. Richard L. Brengle (New York: Appleton-Century-Crofts, 1964) 382.

aware that a simple open man is most receptive when he is mystified, and Merlin delighted in mystery. (*Acts*, 8)

Because of his native wisdom, he becomes adviser to the king, directing him in matters of living with Igrayne to planning battles. King Arthur himself says to Merlin, "'You are a man of marvels. Always you move in mystery like a dream'" (43). Arthur then asks him if he, Arthur, must die in battle. Merlin's response is enigmatic, "'It is God's will that you be punished for your sins'" (43). Of his own death Merlin says that it will be shameful and ugly and ridiculous. Merlin is also capable of magical arts, such as suddenly vanishing from the council of King Lot and the ten kings. In court, Merlin functions as a sage, somewhat like a Samuel Hamilton in *East of Eden* or even one of the reflective paisanos from the Cannery Row trilogy.

For Malory Merlin is not a magician but a mage. He has power and knowledge and clearly identifies the source in God. When he heals Uther, Merlin makes it clear that it is not just within his own power: "'God must have his will. But see that all ye barons come before King Uther in the morning, and God and I shall give him speech" (7). Merlin makes clear under whose authority he operates. It is this positioning, moreover, that makes him the effective adviser—his appointed role in *Logres*—that he is to King Arthur. Like the Old Testament prophet, Merlin has acute knowledge of where things stand in the present and what must be done to satisfy the future. He is the soothsayer—the truth teller.

Return for a moment to his status as mage, a word that connotes far more than mere magician. Morgan Le Fay functions as the latter. In medieval lore, the two differ considerably. The mage has authority; the magician has power. The mage uses authority justly to help others. The magician uses power to get more power at the expense of others. The mage works directly; the magician manipulates intermediary devices. We notice that in the *Morte,* when Morgan seeks to kill Arthur, she sends a damsel with a mantle as a gift. Arthur astutely tells the damsel to put it on first, whereupon she collapses in death. The mantle is the intermediary device. Most importantly, the mage is appointed and gifted to his task. The magician acquires her power by long study in the dark arts of necromancy.

In *The Acts of King Arthur* Steinbeck captures well the destructive nature of Morgan. And here he also gives cause for it: "She became proficient in the dark and destructive magic which is the weapon of the jealous" (119). Jealousy is her root sin, more commonly known as envy. Envy always destroys and perverts to an extent that cannot be repaired. Steinbeck captures this also: "She joyed in bending and warping men to her will through beauty and enchantment, and when these failed she used the blacker arts of treason and murder. It was her pleasure to use men against men, fashioning from their weaknesses weapons for their strength" (119).[13] With these deceits and powers she tries to destroy Arthur. Why? Because she is jealous of his pre-eminence in the kingdom. It must be said that Steinbeck does a splendid piece of work capturing the complex psychological portrait that is Morgan Le Fay. One might think at points that he is describing Cathy Ames.

To Elizabeth Otis, on November 19, 1956, when he was just beginning his work on Arthur, Steinbeck wrote: "I have a feeling this will go very fast—if there aren't too many interruptions. Also, I think that in this I can weather

---

[13] "Their strength" almost certainly has to be an error caused by the incomplete construction of first and second drafts that we now have, posthumously, of *The Acts of King Arthur and His Noble Knights*. Taken in context, the phrase seems to read "fashioning from their weaknesses weapons for *her* strength."

interruptions. I find I know it very well, after all these years."[14] On July 8, 1965, a decade later, he again wrote Otis: "I go struggling along with the matter of Arthur." It is not the purpose of this study to understand why Steinbeck broke his engagement with *Morte*, yet the difficulties in composition mirror the difficulties he found in resolving the warring factions of good and evil, both in Malory's manuscript and his own. The story had ended. While describing the "task of ethics" in his *Beyond Right and Wrong*, Harry Girvetz observes,

> *Particular* moral dilemmas are the stuff of which great novels and dramas are made...but philosophers have all too often been content to leave the examination of such dilemmas to novelists and playwrights...and have neglected to extract generalizations from them that might throw light on the moral life.[15]

One might wonder why this is so. Girvetz responds to the question:

> If one wonders why, the not too flattering answer may be that they have often been primarily concerned with providing an apologetic for one or other system of values or way of life and hence have taken for granted one or other prevailing moral code ideal to the neglect of the situations in which moral codes are reformulated and new ideals actually chosen.[16]

Although we have seen Steinbeck's ethical positioning change over the course of his career, it is true that he shared in Girvetz's description of the novelist's task as dramatizing the conflict between good and evil. That *The Acts of King Arthur*

---

[14] John Steinbeck, "Appendix," *The Acts of King Arthur and His Noble Knights*, 318.

[15] Harry K. Girvetz, *Beyond Right and Wrong: A Study in Moral Theory* (New York: Macmillan, 1973) 145.

[16] Ibid.

bears many artistic excellences, and that with helpful advice from his agent and his editor it might have been a powerful finished product, seems certain. Its final lack of coherence, however, or its simple lack of completion, lies in Steinbeck's failure to comprehend fully Malory's cosmology, or even to construct his own to squeeze the story into. Very likely, this accounts for why Steinbeck could not and did not complete his labor of a decade.

To deal with this rather radical notion, it may be beneficial first to consider several other possible reasons Steinbeck left the work unfinished. On March 1, 1958, Steinbeck reported that he wrote the first lines of the book: This was the opening dedication to his sister Mary. The main body of writing didn't really take place until spring 1959, the intervening period having been spent with reading and research: "Almost by enchantment the words began to flow, a close-reined, taut, economical English, unaccented and unlocalized.... It is just as simple as that and I think it is the best prose I have ever written" (*Acts*, 359). His letters to Otis and Horton in spring 1959 are exultant in much the same vein. Steinbeck took great joy in his writing and also believed it was some of his best. In many ways it was, many passages of the final manuscript show the dedicated task of the master craftsman, that instinct for the right word, the appropriate and telling image. Steinbeck intended several drafts of corrections and emendations, but he believed he had the essence of his project well in hand.

Then, how devastating to hear from your professional advisers that this isn't really what they wanted. In his very long response letter, Steinbeck wrote: "It is natural to look for arguments in my defense or in defense of the work as I am doing it. Let me say first that I hope I am too professional to be shocked into paralysis" (*Acts*, 374). Nonetheless, the letter exudes a deep sense of sadness, even an Arthurian sense of betrayal by close allies. To be sure, there was fault on each side, partially induced by distance. Elizabeth Otis wanted something popular, a big seller. Along with Chase Horton she found the language forced and artificial, but apparently she had done little to make these wishes known to Steinbeck. He, on the other hand, wanted to craft an accessible retelling of the original that would endure beyond any fleeting popularity. And his was a retelling, not a translation.[17] He freely edited and abbreviated repetitive passages in Malory. He tried to reduce the unwieldy range of coincidental battles that Malory, himself a warrior, loved but which in his prose slows scenes to near inertia.

At the same time, however, when he submitted his initial chapters to Otis, it is also clear that she was taken by surprise. A large degree of this is Steinbeck's fault. Apparently he had never submitted a prospective or plan for the work. Instead, he

---

[17] It is likely that Steinbeck had sent the first draft of his *Acts* to Elizabeth Otis and Chase Horton in late April 1959. That draft of 576 pages was later discovered in the Martha Heasley Cox Center for Steinbeck Studies at San Jose State University, as accompanied by a note from Elaine Steinbeck that reads in part:

> To Whom It May Concern:
>
> I really don't know what I have here. Some kind of translation of King Arthur. A bit of it corrected by John [the first 8 pages]. Elizabeth is not alive to tell me if it was used when we published the book, and I no longer remember.

It was not in fact used for the book, for Steinbeck started with a second, more vernacular rendition. In fact, Nancy Stock in her careful comparative study of the two drafts, calls the first a "translation." The second, then, would be a retelling. See Nancy P. Stork, "The Pale and Perfect Measured Parade: The First Draft of Steinbeck's *Acts of King Arthur* at San Jose State University," *The Medieval Forum* 4 (December 2004). This is an online journal at <http://www.sjsu.edu/~medieval/volume4/stork.html>.

wrote of his great joy in living in England, in doing research, and in writing. Two different people, living several thousand miles apart, worked with two entirely different assumptions of what their project entailed. Clearly, however, at that point Steinbeck's enthusiasm for and commitment to the project diminished. He wrote at one point in the letter, "You will understand that what saddened me most was the tone of disappointment in your letter" (*Acts*, 376). But a bit later he adds, "Finally, and I won't labor the point after this, I feel I am reaching toward something valuable" (*Acts*, 377). But his reaching had effectively drawn to an end.

That is precisely the difficulty in evaluating Steinbeck's *Acts* as an ethical work—we don't have the final stories so essential to Malory's cosmology and ethical view. Steinbeck left his retelling with the treachery of Lancelot and Guinevere, clearly the turning point of the story, to which Steinbeck gives a profound psychological depth not found in Malory. Lancelot in the *Morte* is a hearty knight, a worker of great deeds, and a relentless paramour. He had a quick eye for every "fair damsel" and was equally quick to work on his proclivities. When Dame Elaine takes her case to Guinevere, Lancelot "leapt out of a window bereft of his wits" (Malory, 494).

In the *Morte* Lancelot is not simply an impetuous man; he is a sinful man. This becomes clear when he is interrogated by the hermit, a wise and holy man, while Lancelot is on the Grail Quest:

> "Sir," said the good man, "are ye not Sir Lancelot du Lake?"
>
> "Yea, sir," said he.
>
> "Sir, what seek ye in this country?"
>
> "Sir," said Sir Lancelot, "I go to seek the adventures of the Sangreal."
>
> "Well," said he, "Seek it ye well may, but though it were here ye would have no power to see it, any more than a blind

> man could see a bright sword. That is because of your sin; otherwise ye would be more able than any man living." (*Morte,* 562)

Lancelot then wears a hair-shirt as emblem of his guilt and mourning.

The Grail Quest, and Lancelot's denial, place us in a position to make judgments about good and evil, and judgments that simply elude us in Steinbeck's retelling. The denial of the Grail to Lancelot signifies that his sins have not been against humans only, but that they have also disrupted the order of the spheres. Just as his base love for Guinevere ruptures the internal order of Camelot—the *Logres*—so too it violates the divine order on which *Logres* is constructed. The Book of the Sangreal is the high spiritual moment of Malory's story, filled with miraculous signs, revelations, and sacred stories. Here all things are revealed to the searching knights who merit hearing them. Ironically, Galahad, Lancelot's son by King Pell's daughter, receives one of the fullest of such stories.

While in Steinbeck's *Acts* Lancelot experiences sadness over his miscreance, in Malory there is a keen recognition that he has sinned. That is not just against the *comitatus* but against divine order. When Malory's Arthur falls into a vision-haunted coma of twenty-four days and nights, the full spiritual import strikes him:

> But on the twenty-fifth day it befell after midday that he opened his eyes, and when he saw the folk he made great sorrow and said, "Why have ye awakened me? For I was more at ease that I am now. Ah, Jesus Christ, who might be so blessed that he might openly see Thy great marvels of secrecy there where no sinner may be?"
>
> "What have ye seen?" said those about him.

"I have seen," said he, "such marvels that no tongue may tell, and more than any heart may think. And had not my sin been before-time, I would have seen much more."

Then they told him how he had lain there four and twenty days and nights, and he thought it was punishment for the four and twenty years that he had been a sinner. (613)[18]

On this earth, Lancelot realizes, he has followed his own way, not the way of the divine *Logos* incarnated in *Logres*.

Malory's accounting is not chronologically linear. It leaps in and out of scenarios willy-nilly. Almost certainly, however, Malory intends to show that Lancelot's adultery with Guinevere happened after the revelation of his sins. Lancelot cannot escape being Lancelot. But in this woeful scene, where Lancelot's hands are cut to the bone from ripping loose the window bars to the Queen's chamber, he lay in bloody ecstasy throughout the night with Guinevere. Not until he returns to his own chamber at dawn does he have Sir Lavagne tend to his wounds. But the blood he left behind is sure evidence. Sir Malagant spies the blood on Guinevere's bedding and accuses her: "Ah, madame. I now have found you a false traitoress unto my lord Arthur.... Therefore, I will accuse you of treason before my Lord King Arthur" (676). It is treason. Vows have been broken. Arthur's court has been fractured from within. In Malory's accounting it is also sin. Through a network of lies, and his prowess on the battlefield in which he kills his accuser, Lancelot nonetheless lives on. If Lancelot cannot escape being Lancelot, he also cannot escape the essential evil that he is—proud, conniving, deceitful, and a two-fisted sinner. He is the demon unleashed to destroy Arthur's kingdom.

---

[18] Lancelot's comment that "no tongue may tell, and more than any heart may think" echoes 1 Cor 2:9: "No eye has seen, no ear has heard, no mind has conceived what God has prepared for those who love him" (NIV).

None of this gritty reality appears in Steinbeck's *Acts*. In fact, from the course he was taking before he left off, it appears that he was willing to bowdlerize the original to concoct an adventure. The original is not an adventure; it is a quest, from Arthur's vision to create the peaceable kingdom on earth, albeit through mighty acts of war, to having that kingdom survive. If Malory is to be believed, that kingdom of God on earth, the *Logres,* cannot survive. Humans are inherently sinful, disobedient, seeking their own. Lancelot is just such a person. So is Guinevere. Both represent how far humans can fall from some ethical order.

An ethical wrong is such because it violates a just order. It requires justice in the sense of recognition of wrong and recompense or punishment for wrong. The victim here is clearly Arthur. He has been wronged by the infidelity of Lancelot and his queen. But when we remember that Arthur represents divine order as God's representative in the *Logres,* the wrong done disrupts the fundamental order of the universe. Here Malory works out a fitting denouement to his great tale. Lancelot banishes himself from England with a hundred knights in order to take up residence in his native lands. When King Arthur pursues him, Gawain vows to avenge his king upon Lancelot: "I, Sir Gawain, send him [Lancelot] word that I promise him by the faith I owe unto God and to knighthood that I shall never leave him till he hath slain me or I him" (724). Gawain is defeated but not killed in the two ensuing challenges. Arthur returns to England to find Sir Mordred and a hundred thousand warriors arrayed against him. Arthur is placed upon the barge to Avalon; Guinevere forsakes her position for a nunnery. There Lancelot comes to visit her.

Lancelot vows to become a recluse and spend the rest of his days in prayer, especially for Guinevere. The queen responds:

"Ah, Sir Lancelot…if thou wilt do so and hold to thy promise: But I can only believe that thou wilt turn to the world again" (744). When Lancelot visits the bishop to be shriven, he laments, "Who may trust this world?" Again, Malory follows the biblical concept that the world is that entity that stands opposed to the kingdom of God.[19] The world is that dark place where human lusts overcome law and the light of *Logres* fails to shine. One may choose to live in either world. Lancelot attempted to straddle both. Malory shows it cannot be done.

One can only wonder what Steinbeck might have done with the rest of Malory's tale—a powerful ethical study. Steinbeck clearly wanted to focus on a man-centered world, probing the psychology of certain actions and their effects. He was powerfully enamored of Malory himself—his life and his literature—and mentioned several times to Elizabeth Otis that he was writing about Malory. As it stands, *The Acts of King Arthur and His Noble Knights* is precisely that: a series of acts. As adventurous as they may be, as well told as they are, they fail to rise to the level of an ethical treatise that structures an order of why certain acts are right and others wrong, what the consequences of those actions might be, and what just order they uphold or violate.

[19] See especially 1 Corinthians 1, and also Eph 2:2 and 6:12.

7

The Dignity of Humanity

During the decade Steinbeck spent with his magnificent obsession of *The Acts of King Arthur,* he still spent ample time penning short opinion pieces. The titles of several of those he published provide a good indication of the turn of thinking he experienced during the *Morte* years.

I list just a few of these in chronological date of publication:

"Adlai Stevenson and John Steinbeck Discuss the Past and the Present," *Newsday,* 22 December 1959: 34–35.

"Have We Gone Soft?" *New Republic,* 15 February 1960: 11–15.

"In Quest of America," a three-part series published in *Holiday,* July 1961–February 1962.

"The Language of Courtesy," *New World Review,* December 1964: 26.

At the same time he was writing his *Letters to Alicia,* his journalism from the fractious and doomed Vietnam War. Along with these published pieces, there were many short pieces and written reflections while he did his daily warm-up to work on Malory. In many of these one can see a deep sense of questioning about American values. It is not surprising to see many of the issues and subjects rise in *America and Americans,* first published by Viking in 1966.

In a way, however, Steinbeck never left Camelot in writing the book. This was something far different than his essentially benign adventures with Charley. He now sat enthroned, passing judgments on his minions. *America* is an often-scathing indictment of life as he meets it, his jousting in the arena of American values. More significantly, it represents his final transition to deontological ethics, or the ethical ought.

Virtue Ethics

Certain other ethical patterns may pertain to Steinbeck's last decade of work. Stephen K. George, for example, argues the use of virtue ethics—"emphasis upon the actor rather than the action, on issues of individual moral character rather than on ethical principles and duties"—in *East of Eden* and *The Winter of Our Discontent*.[1] According to George, Steinbeck is particularly fruitful for virtue analysis "because he took seriously the emotions, virtues, and vices of his characters" (268). The argument appears to be in serious difficulty at this early point. To say, first of all, that virtues have to do with actors rather than actions seems bizarre. An agent does not stand in isolation, unless (1) he is dead, or (2) there are no other agents. Even a hermit in his isolation still stands *in relation* to define his isolation. Furthermore, because Steinbeck took seriously the "emotions, virtues, and vices of his characters" is not an ethical commentary but an aesthetic one. Finally, even if an aesthetic judgment, it is not demonstratively true. As a non-teleologist, and he remained so for much of his life, Steinbeck aimed to present things, including characters, as they are.

The way to work the virtue ethics, then, is to redefine several fundamental terms. This George does, with guidance

---

[1] Stephen K. George, "The Philosophical Mind of John Steinbeck: Virtue Ethics and His Late Fiction," *The Moral Philosophy of John Steinbeck*, ed. Stephen K. George (Lantham: Scarecrow Press, 2005) 268.

from Justin Oakley, who argues in *Morality and the Emotions* that "emotions are based on certain beliefs and actually move us to do certain things."[2] Beliefs then precede emotions, direct them, tell us how to act upon them. This is essentially basic Aristotelianism, except Aristotle adds the intervening will. More to the point, we ask how beliefs are formed. Not by emotions, so we effectively rule out hedonism. With this Steinbeck would have stood in agreement. But beliefs, and this is the point I believe Steinbeck reached late in his career, are not shaped by emotions. They are instead shaped by mind, experience, and will. Furthermore, if shaped by experience then beliefs occur in actions. The mind cannot be isolated as actor alone. And those actions are willed by nothing more nor less than the belief that an act is to good or evil ends. Finally, virtue ethics is found wanting when applied to Steinbeck.

Teleological Ethics

Deontological ethics might best be understood against the backdrop of teleological theories. William Frankena defines the latter like this:

> The final appeal, directly or indirectly, must be to the comparative amount of good produced, or rather to the comparative balance of good over evil produced. Thus, an act is *right* if and only if it the rule under which it falls produces, will probably produce, or is intended to produce *at least as great a balance of good over evil* as any available alternative; an act is *wrong* if and only if it does not do so. An act *ought to be done* if and only if it or the rule under which it falls produces,

[2] Ibid., 269. See Justin Oakley, *Morality and the Emotions* (New York: Routledge, 1993) and also his *Virtue Ethics and Professional Roles* (Cambridge: Cambridge University Press, 2006).

> will probably produce, or is intended to produce a *greater balance of good over evil* than any available alternative.[3]

The emphasis here is whether the act to be committed promotes the moral good or promotes the greatest balance of good over evil. For example, I can act in a way that brings me great personal pleasure, but I must ask whether it does so at the expense of great harm to others.

Now it should be clear here that no claim for a teleological ethics is being made for Steinbeck, but that we raise the subject only to clarify the universal obligations theory of the deontologist. Before we arrive at that point, however, a further clarification should be made about the term *teleology*, for it answers to both philosophical and literary definitions. As such, we can say that Steinbeck was not an ethical teleologist, but he was a teleological writer. In ethical as well as in critical appraisal we are left with the question, to what end are the stories told? Story as such requires a teleology; the very nature of narrative initiates a progression toward certain ends.

In a particularly helpful study of the ends and purposes of story, "The End of Literature: Reflections on Literature and Ethics," Clarence Walhout works out a synthesis between teleology and ethics in literature. Walhout defines *teleology* in terms altogether applicable to Steinbeck: "Teleology does not require an Aristotelian conception of an ideal or universal *telos* or end or goal. It does not even require that the *telos* be a certain or determinate good. It does imply, however, that living in time entails some sense of purposeful movement toward desired goals."[4] Such a view circumvents the common

---

[3] William Frankena, *Ethics* (New York: Prentice-Hall, 1973) 14.

[4] Clarence Walhout, "The End of Literature: Reflections on Literature and Ethics," *Christianity and Literature* 47 (summer 1998): 459. See also Jeffrey Stout, who in *Ethics after Babel: The Languages of Morals and Their Discontents* (Princeton: Princeton University Press, 2005), similarly argues

understanding of teleology as a fixed or transcendent goal, and thereby outside of human endeavor.

Assuming then that teleology is the pursuit of ends or goals enacted in one's life—and consequently also in one's art—how does this belief affect what we make of ethics in literature? Again, Walhout expands his view in a way that also might apply to Steinbeck:

> Though universal truths and values may be important for the study of literature, the primary purpose of literature is not to convey or represent such truths or values but to explore the possibilities and consequences of specific human actions and thoughts in a narrative situation. Whatever we may mean by universal truths and values in literature, they are qualities that even the end of literature and are not themselves the end. The end is the narration of actions that have ethical significance.... Actions that are narrated in literature are often taken as illustrations of universal truths and values rather than as what they are—the uncertain and often stumbling efforts of characters to find a way to act in a confusing world.[5]

Thereby, as Walhout points out, literature dramatizes for the reader the conflicts and choices universal to the human condition. Literature may be described as a searching out, rather than, a positing, of universal truths or values.[6]

---

that the *telos* need not be "a fixed conception of the good, derived once and for all from a philosophical view of the human essence" (237). For Stout, the *telos* is only worthwhile if it is in fact attainable in human affairs.

[5] Ibid., 461.

[6] In *The Company We Keep: An Ethics of Fiction* (Berkeley: University of California Press, 1988), Wayne C. Booth contends that "[e]very appraisal of narrative is implicitly a comparison between the always complex experience we have had in its presence and what we have known before" (71).

A sense of teleology that is ongoing draws a reader into possibilities the author holds forth. Into a narrative the author provides conflicts and choices that the reader works through, and thereby places his or her own personhood into the possible resolutions or effects of those conflicts and choices. The reader participates in the story. While symbolism may guide possible choices, it is not structured in an exclusively determinative way to admit one choice only. In arriving at an ethical position, then, both artist and reader necessarily work through the ambiguity that grants freedom of choice. Often the work ends in a tension of unresolved options. Nonetheless, that very act of pondering conflicting values, of weighing alternatives, and of abandoning untenable responses constitutes an ethical act.

Deontological Ethics

While little sense of a theological ethics is manifested in Steinbeck's work, an acute sense of right and wrong behavior does appear. When Ma Joad feeds the family stew to starving children, she clearly does the right thing. When the trackers pursue Kino to get the pearl, they do a wrong thing. But no divine being is present to tell us one is right and the other wrong. Instead of a theological ethics, Steinbeck most frequently positions us at a deontological ethics.[7] Instead of asking the familiar ethical question of what is the right or wrong choice, deontological ethics asks where one obtains a sense of rightness or wrongness itself.[8] Is it simply a utilitarian pattern (what would bring about the most good for the most

---

[7] My summary of deontological ethics here is necessarily brief. Several of the best introductions to the philosophy include Nancy Davis's "Contemporary Deontology," Charles Fried's *Right and Wrong*, and John Rawls' *A Theory of Justice*, and W. D. Ross's *The Right and the Good*.

[8] The term *deontology* derives from the Greek *deon* (duty) and *logos* (knowledge or science). Hence the knowledge of duty.

people) or a cultural norm? If one feels that certain acts are right (compassion for the needy) and certain others are wrong (genocide of a needy people), how do we know we ought to do one and not the other? To extend the issue, why do we see the genocidal tyrant as an aberration of some moral quality, not just doing wrong but being evil? Deontological ethics begins with an investigation of where the "oughtness" behind right and wrong human actions originates. In our case, the question becomes *How do we know that pride is wrong and compassion is good?* Steinbeck suggests at the simplest level that we as humans share our lives with fellow humans. We live in community; therefore we ought not harm others.

The modern shaping of deontological ethics occurred in Immanuel Kant's *The Critique of Practical Reason,* a response to his own *Pure Reason* which shaped his epistemology by marrying reason and experience but left no room for "oughtness," or what he calls the "Categorical Imperative," the "thou ought." Humanity needs this to make sense and order out of life, to validate an ethical existence. Therefore, Kant postulates these universals derived from his Categorical Imperative: that everyone has freedom to seek the universal; that everyone has a soul that is free and that seeks; and that this soul has an underlying cause that is God. The cause of human knowledge in ethical choices, unlike Pure Reason, lies outside of the natural world.

For the deontologist, ethical values are not merely good suggestions; they are obligations morally required of us. The right act, then, is to say this ought to be done. But how do we know that? One option derives from H. A. Pritchard's 1909 essay, "Does Moral Philosophy Rest on a Mistake?" in which he argues that we apprehend what we ought to do intuitively. We can see immediately or intuitively that certain actions are right without having to examine these acts as utilitarian. The source of "oughtness," then, is intuition, an innate quality of human nature itself. One can see the correspondence between Pritchard's and Kant's views but also sense that each leaves a problem. If this sense of oughtness originates in human nature, then the "right thing" is not always clear, which is where we often find Steinbeck's characters ethically positioned. In response to Kant and Pritchard, however, others attempt to correct the intrinsic ambiguity by the standard of "disinterestedness." We are to be interested in the consequences of our actions upon others; we are disinterested in that we refuse to allow personal interests to outweigh the good of others. Beyond question, Steinbeck explored the nooks and crevices of human nature, bringing the hidden to light, exposing lies and fabrications, and exploring the costs of pursuing prideful ends. Such qualities in and of themselves might warrant the appellation of a "moral writer." But it was not Steinbeck's aim to reduce these investigations to a set of axiomatic truths or didactic principles.

America and Americans

The book came into being circumstantially. Thomas H. Guinzburg of Viking Press had commissioned photographs from across the nation. Wanting to frame them in a book as representative of the nation, he asked Steinbeck to write an introductory essay. As often happened with Steinbeck, however, once he got into a project it tended to explode exponentially. The introductory chapter became nine chapters, plus a foreword and afterword, and the collection of photographs was broken down into supportive portfolios for each chapter. The essays performed a valuable service for Steinbeck at least. Having recently written about his adventures with Charley, using a form in which particulars accrete in episodic fashion, *America* provided the broad sweep that permitted him both to write about and to comment upon.

At times *America* nearly resembles *Travels with Charley* as Steinbeck lets his imagination roam through history and recollections. Like *Charley* also, early chapters often have representative voices, people he met and conversations he recalled. In his sweeping judgments on how we ought to act, however, he often echoes Camelot: "In reviewing our blessings we must pay heed to our leadership."[9] "E Pluribus Unum," the sweeping introduction on the gathering of people and cultures, ends with a parallel to *Morte*. Instead of throwing Excalibur into the lake, however, in the Native-American story Steinbeck integrates, Jimmy throws a fresh trout to the woman in the lake.

The echoes of Camelot only frame the story, for although it was very much alive in Steinbeck's mind, he forces his way toward an orderly analysis of and answer to the question *What is an American?* At several points the account is abrasive, such as the case with the American Indian and also with slavery—as well it should be. In a sense Steinbeck weaves a tapestry of national wrongs. They continue to the present and will in the future:

> Psychoanalysts remind their little patients that they must find the real "me." The real "me" invariably turns out to be a savage, self-seeking little beast. Indeed, if the experts expected

---

[9] John Steinbeck, *America and Americans and Selected Nonfiction*, ed. Susan Shillinglaw and Jackson J. Benson (New York: Viking Press, 2002) 342. Apart from the pleasing addition of samples of Steinbeck's prose throughout his career, this is the only acceptable hardcover printing of *America and Americans*. Originally released in 8-point text on a 35.5 pica line, the text was nearly unreadable. Worse, the text of 52 pages was scattered among 153 pages of photographs.

> to be paid by the patient, rather than by the harassed parents, the couches would be empty.
>
> The foregoing is not a diatribe; it is an exact description of what has been happening to Americans, and it doesn't work in that it does not create adults. Actually, the whole American approach to the young has extended adolescence far into the future, so that very many Americans have never and can never become adults. What has caused this? (372)

Steinbeck winces at the whole modern temperament of entitlement. This tone persists for the majority of the book, where Steinbeck explores American history, then locates and identifies a present example of the ethical wrong. His interest, however, lies less with solutions than with demonstrations. Alternative strategies or means of healing are not always clearly stated. Toward the close of the book, however, Steinbeck does shift directions. His essay on Americans and the land, and on America and the future have enduring worth.

The Land

Only in recent years has critical attention turned toward Steinbeck's environmental beliefs, spurred largely by the three-day conference on those beliefs held on Nantucket Island in May 1992. *Steinbeck and the Environment: Interdisciplinary Approaches* collected the essays from the conference and published them in 1997. Although the scholarly interest in a connected focus came rather late, Steinbeck's environmental views may be traced to the early 1930s and *The Sea of Cortez.* "Environmentalism" has meant different things during different eras. Joel Hedgpeth, a near contemporary of Steinbeck, reflects on the changing definitions:

> Environmentalism, as we know it today, is based on the realization that the human race is exceeding the earth's capacity at an exponential rate by overpopulation and that

> continued exploitation of the earth's resources to support our elaborate material culture is not sustainable. Used in this sense, the term "environmentalism" did not come into common use until the observation of the first Earth Day on 21 April 1970. John Steinbeck died on 20 December 1968, about fourteen months earlier. Nevertheless, our generation (I include myself as well as Steinbeck, since I am only nine years and eight months younger) began to hear about concern for protection of natural resources fairly early on. The word then was conservation....[10]

If one were to trace Steinbeck's career in regard to the environment one would find a deep and pervasive concern for how humans interact with the land.

In *America and Americans* Steinbeck traces our failure in regard to the environment to a perfidious irresponsibility with its roots in the spirit of humanity. While in modern environmental ethics we are inclined to see irresponsibility in terms of criminal actions—that is, littering is a criminal act punishable by a fine, as is toxic waste dumping—Steinbeck sees this irresponsibility as a failure in understanding and sympathy. While littering may not have been, in his time, a criminal action, it was an evil action nonetheless. The distinction is important to the case here, for evil, in Steinbeck's ethics, is a positioning of the heart in regard to other living things. We either devour those things like tigers, as *Cannery Row* had it, or live with them in a respectful equilibrium.

The history of Americans in regard to the land, in Steinbeck's view, is marked by a rapacious attitude that sees the land merely as something to be used or abused. Obsessed with the notion that the land was limitless, early settlers

---

[10] Joel Hedgpeth, "John Steinbeck: Late-Blooming Environmentalist," *Steinbeck and the Environment: Interdisciplinary Approaches*, ed. Susan F. Beegel, et al. (Tuscaloosa: University of Alabama Press, 1997) 294.

"abandoned their knowledge of kindness to the land in order to maintain its usefulness" (379). Implicitly whatever was not useful could be cast aside to get at what was useful.

But as Grandfather testified in "Leader of the People" (written in 1934) in *The Red Pony,* we have learned that the land is not limitless. We have learned that the land is fragile, that the gouges of our rapacious greed forever mar its face, that taking its hidden treasures always leaves an irreparable scar. We have learned that it is susceptible to decimation and deterioration. We have learned our evil toward the land. When one acquires such knowledge, Steinbeck asserts, a pressure of outrage grows.

It must be admitted that in *America and Americans* Steinbeck does a better job of delineating problems than of offering practical solutions. So too in regard to his environmental ethic. Outrage is an important part of an ethical consideration; it constitutes, in fact, the basic premise of an ethic, for an ethic is always and ultimately incarnated in action. An ethical person acts against a perceived evil; one who ignores it may be said to be ethically culpable for the evil itself. To do nothing is to permit; to permit is to condone. Steinbeck's own ethical action is the work of revelation: to make readers mindful of our despoliation of the land. In regard to a specific program to rectify that course, however, this ethic, at least as delineated in *America and Americans,* is found wanting.

Steinbeck arrays several examples of when a people's outrage led to actions, as when a California highway route was changed to avoid a stand of redwoods, but most frequently his response in *America and Americans* is formulated as a fond reminiscence for the way things once were, a profound regret for the way they are, and a tempered hope for better times ahead.

From his earliest years Steinbeck was exploring an ethical attitude—a pattern of right living—basing upon a belief in the possibility of a harmonious relationship between humanity and the environment. If one approaches the land in a self-interested way, the result will inevitably be despoliation and depletion of what it means to be human. Humanity and the environment are linked in a delicate interplay. Respect for this linkage, seeing the land as it is in its own right, as a living and delicate thing, not only ennobles humanity and ultimately liberates humanity but also grants self-knowledge and validation through a loving and harmonious relationship between humanity and the land.

The Future

America and Americans is set up like a row of rhetorical dominos. Each chapter acquires weight and topples into the final where we face the timeless ethical question: How then shall we live? The question leads Steinbeck to a bleak pessimism:

> First, let us try to find something to call this subtle and deadly illness. Immorality does not describe it, nor does lack of integrity, nor does dishonesty. We might coin the word "anethics," but that would be too scholarly an approach to a subject that is far more dangerous than anything that has happened to us. It is a creeping, evil thing that is invading every cranny of our political, our economic, our spiritual, and our psychic life. I begin to think that the evil is one thing, not many. (392)

Having just recalled many "good old days" in preceding chapters, Steinbeck nonetheless asserts,

> I'm not going to preach about any good old days. By our standards of comfort they were pretty awful. What did they have then that we are losing or have lost? Well, for one thing

> they had rules—rules concerning life, limb, and property, rules governing deportment, manners, conduct, and rules defining dishonesty, dishonor, misconduct, and crime. The rules were not always obeyed but they were believed in, and breaking them was savagely punished. (393)

Where does this sense of "rules" come from? Steinbeck recognizes that at one time they had their source in God, but that case no longer holds. That changed to a general perception of deontological oughtness, "the rules were understood and accepted by everyone" (394). In the modern age, however, the rules constantly have to be rewritten.

It has been said there are no new vices; we have just shown far greater imagination in condoning vice. T. S. Eliot's puzzled Gerontion considers that, "Virtues/ Are forced upon us by our impudent crimes."[11] Virtue becomes relative to the age. Actions that were abhorrent a hundred years past become accepted practice. Are virtues then the products of an age? If Steinbeck were still holding his non-teleological ethics, he would have to answer *yes*. That's the way things are. Ethics are descriptive, not prescriptive. He can no longer hold such a view; his passionate involvement in America changed him fully as much as his passionate pursuit of Camelot. His concluding chapter is not merely a broadside, nor an accusatory indictment, although it is both of those to a certain degree. Rather, it is a lamentation, a prophetic one in which the writer mourns the present state, sees the way the people should go, but seems powerless to drive them in a new direction.

Steinbeck confesses, "It is hard to criticize the people one loves. I knew this would be a painful thing to write. But I am far from alone in my worry. My mail is full of it—letters of anxiety. The newspapers splash so much of it that perhaps we

---

[11] T. S. Eliot, "Gerontion," *Collected Poems 1909–1962* (New York: Harcourt, Brace World, 1970) 30.

have stopped seeing" (395). Perhaps the only way to redirect the people, to help them find their love of the land and the people, is to have the prophet point a burning finger at the wrongs of the nation. The symptoms of one national ethical crisis are clear. Steinbeck identifies these as anxiety, nervousness, and sadness. As he turns to causes, he asserts, "I strongly suspect that our moral and spiritual disintegration grows out of our lack of experience with plenty" (396). And as a close kin to plenty, "We are poisoned with things." Things are expendable; they break, they wear out, they get lost, yet we build the actions of our lives on acquiring those very things. In this lies the etiology of our wrong deeds:

> It is probable that the want of things and the need of things have been the two greatest stimulants toward the change and complication we call progress. And surely we Americans, most of us starting with nothing, have contributed our share of wanting. Wanting is probably a valuable human trait. It is the means of getting that can be dangerous. (396)

The desire for things is the immediate cause of our ethical devolution.

This is hardly a new supposition, and one that is demonstrable by the rise and fall of empires throughout history. The important issue is whether Steinbeck sees any way to stave off the decline, to pull the blind man back from the cliff's edge. The problem ethically is that the way of life he laments is not just a turning from the deontological ethics he champions, although it does do that, but it supplants those ethics with an entire way of life that sees no need for them. If one desires things, one desires them for the individual self, not the community. As Steinbeck sees the moral problem, these become my things, my plenty, even at the expense of the commonweal. And if that is the case, where the arrogant individual stands over and against the commonweal, the latter will suffer as a whole. The towers of Camelot soon come tumbling down.

If an excess of goods and the desire for things create two foundational diseases in the body of Steinbeck's ethics, the third is the lack of a vision that grants us purpose. Again, a reader might well pick up resonances of *Morte D'Arthur* here, with Malory's vision of the *Logres* and the validating Grail Quest. Steinbeck finds no such vision. As a growing nation we had pursued dreams and goals; now we appear in a hurry to get nowhere.

> We have the things and we have not had time to develop a way of thinking about them. We struggle with our lives in the present and our practices in the long and well-learned past. We have had a million years to get used to the idea of fire and only twenty to prepare ourselves for the productive-destructive tidal wave of atomic fission. We have more food than we can use and no way to distribute it.... We retire men and women at the age of their best service for no other reason than that we need their jobs for younger people. To allow ourselves the illusion of usefulness we have standby crews for functions which no longer exist. We manufacture things we do not need and try by false and vicious advertising to create a feeling of need for them. We have found no generally fulfilling method for employing our leisure. To repeat—we have not had time to learn inside ourselves the things that have happened to us. (398)

This third part of the lamentation over ethical ills is not new for Steinbeck. As recently as *Charley* he recoiled from the thick flow of traffic and returned to the blue highways. As early as Peter Randall's desperate attempt to escape "The Harness" (written in 1934), from *The Long Valley* stories, it was there also. We are all, as Steinbeck has it, people enslaved by time and hurrying desperately and pointlessly to escape it.

Ethical Response

It is easy to decry a perceived wrong; it can be very hard to act on it. But perhaps the hardest task is to think through it and propose answers. Without that last task, *America and Americans* would be a vindictive diatribe, a screed against perceived but unavoidable evils, yet out of the negative Steinbeck excavates some answers to the nation's need. In a transitional paragraph, Steinbeck encapsulates his view of where we presently stand:

> I have named the destroyers of nations: comfort, plenty, and security—out of which grow a bored and slothful cynicism, in which rebellion against the world as it is and myself as I am are submerged in listless self-satisfaction. A dying people tolerates the present, rejects the future, and finds its satisfactions in past greatness and half-remembered glory. A dying people arms itself with defensive weapons and with mercenaries against change. When greatness recedes, so does belief in greatness. A dying people invariably concedes that poetry has gone, that beauty has withered away. (400–401)

Out of this very stultification, he sees a new restlessness being born. Not surprisingly, it grows among young Americans, who are "rebellious, angry, searching like terriers near a rat's nest" (401).

This was the 1960s, era of restless change fomented by young people. There was radical revolution in their universities, demonstrations on their streets. They claimed certain rights and privileges denied them under the status quo and rioted in the streets to make their message heard. They dropped out of "normal" society, and inhabited a world of Woodstock. They were drafted by the military and sent to fight in a tiny country they had never heard of, in a war that nobody wanted and that we appeared to be losing in staggering defeat. In this cataclysmic era, Steinbeck sensed something of the rebellion against the old codification of rules that signaled change. "Wasted energy," he wrote, "is only a little problem, compared to its lack" (401). And America had grown very, very lazy.

If the energy and rebellion of youth is one quality that gives Steinbeck hope for the future, a second is the discovery of new boundaries to probe and explore. The difficulty in America, he has asserted, is that we are content where we are. We are no longer seekers; we have no grails to pursue. Opening the doors to the future is the powerful force of creativity. Here, in a time-studied sense, Steinbeck resurrects the mantra of *The Sea of Cortez*, for the creative thinker is always guided not just by how things are but by "it might be so." All the world about us lies open to creative investigation:

> In our prehistory—only now beginning to open its cloak a little—we have set a guard of secrecy and holiness on the unknown. The forest, the sky—the unconceivable large, the unseeable small—we once placed beyond our reach in mystery; taboo to approach, forbidden to inspect. Our dreams we gave to ancestors, cantankerous and selfish and dead, while our closest and most precious possession we gave into the hands of God or gods, not kindly or wise, but vain and jealous and greedy—in the image not of ourselves but of the ugly things, precarious and usurped, that power makes of us. Here is a world or a universe unknown, even unconceived of, and perhaps at last open for exploration: the great and mysterious mind and soul of man, a land full of marvels. (401)

We have the gift of creativity. We have abused it to create a world of things. The counterpart is to free creativity to explore not only the hidden secrets of nature, but also those of "the mind and soul" of men.

Steinbeck does not end his study with a singing note of optimism or a clear and compelling ethical creed. The apt term may be "counter-behavior," how we should behave to liberate ourselves from the chains of plenty, the desire for things, and the loss of a national and individual vision. To lean upon the rebellious spirit of the young, to demand for change, and to employ a creative vision, may be practical responses. They also sound suspiciously like political caveats, exhorting people to another new vision.

But are these ethical responses? In a deontological ethic we can agree with Steinbeck that the ailments he locates in American society are ethical wrongs. Why? Because they are self-reflexive and either ignore community or exist at the expense of community. As Steinbeck points out, if I have plenty, my aim is to protect the plenty I have or to add to it. It is an I-centered enterprise. If I desire things, it is so that they may be *my* things. If I fail to encourage a new vision, it is either because I am content with the present state of affairs and the plentitude it has afforded me or I actively discourage change because it threatens my status. But to suggest a spirit of rebellion and vision of creativity is not an adequate ethical apology.

Steinbeck's conclusion, then, and necessarily so, is moving but ethically deferential:

> Americans do not lack places to go and new things to find. We have cut ourselves off from the self-abuse of war by raising it from sin to an extinction. Far larger experiences are open to our restlessness—the fascinating unknown is everywhere. How will the Americans act and react to a new set of circumstances for which new rules must be made? We know from our past some of the things we will do. We will make many mistakes; we always have. We are in the perplexing period of change. We seem to be running in all directions at once—but we are running. And I believe that our history, our experience in America, has endowed us for the change that is coming. We have never sat still for long; we have never been content with a place, a building—or with ourselves. (401–02)

Essentially, Steinbeck fails his own aim by failing to tell us what one ought to do. No writer is forced to be hortatory, not

may be summarized in two key terms. Indifference is an attitude that demeans and diminishes human life. Injustice is an act that impedes another human's privilege to lead a fulfilling life. One can see these pronounced attitudes already in the fiction of the 1930s. In relation to these works, a curious sidebar appeared when in 1938 a graduate student at Ohio University named Merle Danford wrote a master's thesis on Steinbeck's work. Apart from the fact that it was the first graduate thesis written on Steinbeck's work—which included *Tortilla Flat, In Dubious Battle, Of Mice and Men,* and the just recently released *The Long Valley*—the surprising fact is that Steinbeck engaged in a correspondence with the student about his work. It was surprising because Steinbeck was well into the brutal pace he set for himself to write *The Grapes of Wrath.* Clearly, Steinbeck lost patience at times: "Look: this is too complicated. I just write stories."[2]

Surely he did more than that. Every writer writes a piece of him or herself. In the correspondence this surfaces abruptly, almost unintentionally. Steinbeck concluded the questionnaire-interview with a partly apologetic note: "And as to the question as to what I mean by—or what my philosophy is—I haven't the least idea. And if I told you one, it wouldn't be true. I don't like people to be hurt or hungry or unnecessarily sad. It's just about as simple as that."[3] That is as precise a statement of what Steinbeck ethically opposes as he ever gave. Indifference and injustice bear exactly the results Steinbeck dislikes: people hurt, hungry, or unnecessarily sad.

---

[2] Robert DeMott, "Voltaire Didn't Like Anything: A 1939 Interview with John Steinbeck," *Steinbeck Quarterly* 19.1, 2 (Winter–Spring 1986): 8. Reprinted in *Conversations with John Steinbeck,* ed. Thomas Fensch (Jackson: University Press of Mississippi, 1988) 21–27.

[3] Ibid., 10.

The triumphant achievement of *The Grapes of Wrath* lies in Steinbeck's ability to dramatize indifference and injustice and to posit ethical alternatives to them. The Bank and the landowners are amorphous, soulless entities, clearly indifferent to the human lives their actions affect. Joe Davis's boy on his caterpillar tractor and protected by his rubber mask moves like an alien invader over the land. A tenant farmer questions him:

> "Well, what are you doing this kind of work for—against your own people?"
>
> "Three dollars a day. I got damn sick of creeping for my dinner—and not getting it. I got a wife and kids. We got to eat. Three dollars a day, and it comes every day.
>
> "That's right," the tenant said. "But for your three dollars a day fifteen or twenty families can't eat at all. Nearly a hundred people have to go out and wander on the roads for your three dollars a day. Is that right?
>
> And the driver said, "Can't think of that. Got to think of my own kids." (50)

Joe Davis's boy is spokesman for the Bank, indifferent to the needs of the people whose way of life he destroys. His final words to the tenant famer: "And that reminds me...you better get out soon. I'm going through the dooryard after dinner" (51).

The ethical antithesis to the indifferent taking by the Bank is manifested in Ma Joad's spirit of sharing. Several instances stand out. One of the great threats of the displaced, as the tenant farmer points out, is hunger. Ma Joad is a nurturer, exemplified most prominently in her "feeder" scenes, discussed in chapter 3. The most powerful scene occurs in their first campground. The family has been complaining how hungry they are, and Ma Joad prepares a hearty stew. As it is being cooked, a ring of famished children draws in around the stewpot: "The children were embarrassed to be there, but they did not go" (344). It is as if the odor itself could nourish them. As she begins to ladle out the stew to her family, the children's greedy, desperate eyes seem to feed off each plate. "'I dunno what to do,' Ma says. 'I can't rob the fambly. I got to feed the fambly'" (351). Finally she resolves the issue by setting the kettle out, telling them to find a flat stick of wood, and letting them eat. This was not a moral act, done according to some code. In fact, a realistic ethical code might call it immoral since it withheld food from her own famished family. Neither was it a particularly virtuous act; none of the children could possibly get enough to sate their hunger. Nowhere in the novel for that matter is Ma Joad depicted as a woman of great virtue. She can turn on Pa with a tire iron, is strong and enduring, but she is thoroughly pragmatic and will do what it takes to keep the family together. Rather, feeding the children is a deontological act. Ma Joad, unlike the Bank or landowners, believes that starving children ought to be fed.

In "The Consequentialist Perspective" Philip Pettit offers this definition of "rightness": "I shall assume that what is involved in designating something as right, as surface semantics suggests, is a belief that it is right—a cognitive state of ascribing the property of rightness to it."[4] Ma Joad is not a cipher, an undistinguishable nought, in Steinbeck's canon. She endures precisely because she acts upon what she believes is right and lives in singular harmony with that belief. If her world is darkened by the ethical wrongs of indifference and injustice, she nonetheless acts to make a difference and to establish justice.

---

[4] Philip Pettit, "The Consequentialist Perspective," *Three Methods of Ethics: A Debate,* ed. Marcia W. Baron, Philip Pettit, and Michael Slote (Malden MA: Blackwell Publishing, 1997) 103.

These two glimmering ethical beliefs are not confined to Steinbeck's masterpiece. For a time, they nearly blink out during the often desolate and lonely fiction of the 1940s. After his success with *Tortilla Flat,* a charming tragicomedy where one cries with tears of laughter to allay the tears of sorrow, Steinbeck revisited the now-blighted landscape in *Cannery Row* (1945). But here no one emerges to alleviate the creeping horror that Steinbeck sees as modern civilization. When the boy Andy looks into the eyes of the Chinaman in chapter 4, he looks into the infinite abyss of human loneliness: "And the loneliness—the desolate cold aloneness of the landscape made Andy whimper because there wasn't anybody at all in the world and he was left. Andy shut his eyes so he wouldn't have to see it any more" (24). Andy sees a world without a Ma Joad in it.

It seems at first, as Steinbeck suggests, that "Mack and the boys avoid the trap, walk around the poison, step over the noose while a generation of trapped, poisoned, and trussed-up men scream at them" (15). So it seems at first, but their own world becomes addled with the poison and proves inescapable and irremediable. The monster of civilization, by which Steinbeck means an indifferent and unjust body, not only threatens from without but also from within the fragile *comitatus*. The laughter in *Cannery Row* is nervous and thin. No real exigency appears to battle the darkness.

One is not surprised that Steinbeck revisits some of his harshest marine imagery in *Cannery Row*. At the outset Steinbeck establishes the analogy between Cannery Row and the tidal pool that will never be far from the context. "When you collect marine animals," he writes, "there are certain flat worms so delicate that they are almost impossible to capture whole, for they break and tatter under the touch" (3). The statement applies to the author diving deeply into the lives of the characters, but also their fragility when examined too closely. This same fragility translates to their position before the force of civilization. We obtain a second glance into the tidal pool when Doc goes collecting with Hazel, and this time the waters teem with violent action:

> Here a crab tears a leg from his brother. The anemones expand like soft and brilliant flowers, inviting any tired and perplexed animal to lie for a moment in their arms, and when some small crab or little tide-pool Johnnie accepts the green and purple invitation, the petals whip in, the stinging cells shoot tiny narcotic needles into the prey and it grows weak and perhaps sleepy while the searing caustic digestive acids melt its body down. (31)

Like the attractive anemone, civilization too will hold out its temptations to these denizens of Cannery Row. They cannot escape; they have no one but themselves to rely on. The passage in *Cannery Row* darkens commensurately to a hard, vicious pulse of words charged with murderous urgency: "Then the creeping murderer, the octopus, steals out, slowly, softly, moving like a gray mist, pretending now to be a bit of weed, now a rock, now a lump of decaying meat while its evil goat eyes watch coldly" (31). From the creamy foam of waves, Steinbeck has led the reader to a world surcharged by feral, predatory language and actions that malignantly typify any civilization—particularly the war years during which the novel was written—and surely not excluding the Row itself. It was a world starved for some ethical order.

Steinbeck found it by looking back. *Travels with Charley* represented a renewal of self, a journey outward and a journey inward. It led him to the question whether enduring moral virtues can exist. Is it possible to shape a community that returns good for good and that insists upon justice for infractions upon a neighbor's effort to seek the good? In this case, we define the good as basic requirements for being human. To use the examples given in this chapter, we would say that the good for the Joads and the Okies generally as example of a disenfranchised people is both freedom from and freedom for. They merit, as fellow human beings, freedom from the indifferent persecution of the landowners and the banks. They merit freedom from the injustice of tumbling wages and mountains of good fruit being burned while they wander hungry in search of work.

In *Reciprocity* Lawrence C. Becker defines the thesis of his study like this:

> This is a book of moral theory about reciprocity. Its destination is the following set of propositions. Reciprocity is a moral virtue. We ought to be disposed, as a matter of moral obligation, to return good in proportion to the good we receive, and to make reparation for the harm we have done. Moreover, reciprocity is a fundamental virtue. Its requirements have presumptive priority over many competing considerations, and that priority makes reciprocity a crucial consideration for a wide variety of important moral problems.[5]

Becker adds to his definition: "The argument offered in support of these propositions is virtue-theoretic. It is not directly about obligations, rights, duties, interests, preferences, values, or social welfare. Instead it is about excellence of character; it proposes part of a substantive theory of the virtues."[6] That excellence of character Steinbeck sought in *Travels with Charley*. He did not find it. What he found was humanity, alternatively noble and generous, and then mean-spirited and selfish.

To this point, almost without exception, Steinbeck sought ethical premises with the novelist's eye—objective, realistically

---

[5] Lawrence C. Becker, *Reciprocity* (New York: Routledge & Kegan Paul, 1986) 3.

[6] Ibid.

reporting what he saw, naturalistic in his presuppositions. He saw the outward behaviors. Saddened and bewildered by what he witnessed, he accepted those behaviors as the end state of humanity. The great change, signaled by his work on Malory, occurred with the probing questions of why those behaviors exist and what might change them. Already in *East of Eden* he had studied how the inward character of Cathy Ames resulted in vicious wrongs. She harmed others. Like some predatory monster she excavated the secrets of others and threatened them with it. Steinbeck's alternative became a grander dream.

All humanity is arranged like a *comitatus* in Arthur's court.[7] The leader now is not the dilapidated Danny or Mack from the boys on the Row, but one inspirited by knowledge of right and wrong (the *Logres*), one peculiarly gifted to his task of leadership (the sword Excalibur) and one assisted by prophetic counselors (Merlin). But this relationship also prompts obligations for the people: loyalty, fidelity, trust, and actions in accord with the ruler's high ideals.

Steinbeck's high vision of right rule and reciprocating obligations may be a fantasy ideal. It probably was and remains such today, but while studying *Morte D'Arthur* and investigating *America and Americans,* Steinbeck's vision turned increasingly inward, searching for not just the *what* but the *why* of what he perceived as America's moral failure. Although harsh and nearly dyspeptic at times, he appears convinced that a return to right rule and an agreement to obligations could work a renewal in the ethical posture of Americans.

In his study *The Moral Sense,* James Q. Wilson cites four examples of primary qualities of right behavior: sympathy,

---

[7] Steinbeck himself appeared to have found this with the democratic party, particularly Adlai Stevenson with whom Steinbeck felt he could confide his deepest political feelings—particularly his trenchant animosity toward Richard Nixon.

fairness, self-control, and duty.[8] Although noting that some important qualities—courage, modesty, integrity—are either missing or subsumed under the primary qualities, these four, Wilson argues, a common sense of right behavior. In the course of our argument we would call them deontological. It does not seem to me too far a stretch to say that these were also precisely the qualities that Steinbeck longed for in his later years. For him they were not mere fantasy. They were attainable by several clear steps: first, the installation of worthy leaders, those who incarnated ethical ideals rather than pragmatic politics; second, a renewed sense of duty among Americans to such leaders; third, the replacement of things, the devastating avarice, with a commitment to help the needy. Just how these were to be executed Steinbeck found himself at a loss to say. In that respect, he was ever the brilliant novelist that he was, showing but not telling. In that respect also his naturalist vision endured to the end.

[8] See James Q. Wilson, *The Moral Sense* (New York: Macmillan Free Press, 1993) 293.

Bibliography

Allee, W. C. *Animal Aggregations*. Chicago: University of Chicago Press, 1931.

Antico, John. "A Reading of Steinbeck's 'Flight.'" *Modern Fiction Studies* 11.1 (Spring 1965): 45–53.

Aristotle. *Nicomachean Ethics*. Translated by R. D. Hicks. Indianapolis: Bobbs-Merrill, 1962.

———. *De Partibus Animalium, Aristotle Selections*. Edited by W. D. Ross. New York: Charles Scribner's Sons, 1955.

Astro, Richard. *John Steinbeck and Edward F. Ricketts: The Shaping of a Novelist*. Minneapolis: The University of Minnesota Press, 1973.

Baron, Marcia W., Philip Pettit, Michael Slote. *Three Methods of Ethics: A Debate*. Madden MA: Blackwell, 1997.

Becker, Lawrence C. *Reciprocity*. New York: Routledge & Kegan Paul, 1986.

Benson, Jackson J. *The True Adventures of John Steinbeck, Writer*. New York: Viking Press, 1984.

———. "The Background to the Composition of *The Grapes of Wrath*." *Critical Essays on Steinbeck's "The Grapes of Wrath."* Edited by John Ditsky. Boston: G. K. Hall, 1989: 51–74.

Booth, Wayne C. *The Company We Keep*. Berkeley: University of California Press, 1988.

Braswell, William. *Melville's Religious Thought: An Essay in Interpretation*. Durham: Duke University Press, 1943.

Bredahl, A. Carl. *Melville's Angles of Vision*. Gainesville: University of Florida Press, 1972.

Brennan, Joseph Gerard. *Ethics and Morals*. New York: Harper & Row, 1973.

Buell, Lawrence. "In Pursuit of Ethics." *PMLA* 114.1 (January 1999): 7–11.

Camus, Albert. *The Myth of Sisyphus*. Translated by Justin O'Brien. New York: Vintage Books, 1955.

Chaucer, Geoffrey. *The Complete Poetry and Prose of Geoffrey Chaucer*. Edited by John H. Fisher. New York: Holt, Rinehart and Winston, 1989.

DeMott, Robert J. *Steinbeck's Reading: A Catalogue of Books Owned and Borrowed*. New York: Garland, 1984.

———. *Steinbeck's Typewriter: Essays on His Art*. Troy NY: Whitston Publishing, 1996.

———. "Voltaire Didn't Like Anything: A 1939 Interview with John Steinbeck." *Steinbeck Quarterly* 19.1–2 (Winter–Spring 1986): 5–11. Reprinted in *Conversations with John Steinbeck*. Edited by Thomas Fensch. Jackson: University Press of Mississippi, 1988.

———. "'Working at the Impossible': Moby-Dick's Presence in *East of Eden*." *Steinbeck and the Environment: Interdisciplinary Approaches*. Edited by Susan F. Beegel, Susan Shillinglaw, and Wesley N. H. Tiffney, Jr. Tuscaloosa: University of Alabama Press, 1997: 211–28.

Eliot, T. S. "Gerontion." *Collected Poems 1909–1962*. New York: Harcourt, Brace & World, 1970.

Finnis, John. *Fundamentals of Ethics*. Washington DC: Georgetown University Press, 1983.

Frankena, William. *Ethics*. 2nd edition. Englewood Cliffs: Prentice-Hall, 1973.

French, Warren. "Steinbeck's Winter Tale," *Modern Fiction Studies* 11.1 (Spring 1965): 66–74.

Fried, Charles. *Right and Wrong*. Cambridge: Harvard University Press, 1978.

George, Stephen K. "The Disintegration of a Man: Moral Integrity in *The Winter of Our Discontent*." *The Moral Philosophy of John Steinbeck*. Edited by Stephen K. George. Lantham MD: Scarecrow Press, 2005: 161–182.

———. "The Philosophical Mind of John Steinbeck's Virtue Ethics and His Late Fiction." *The Moral Philosophy of John Steinbeck*. Edited by Stephen K. George. Lantham MD: Scarecrow Press, 2005: 266–276.

Gert, Bernard. *Morality: Its Nature and Justification*. New York: Oxford University Press, 1998.

Girvetz, Harry. *Beyond Right and Wrong: A Study in Moral Theory*. New York: Macmillan Free Press, 1973.

Goetz, Steward and Charles Taliaferro. *Naturalism*. Grand Rapids: Wm. B. Eerdmans, 2008.

Han, John J. "'I Want to Make 'Em Happy:' Utilitarian Philosophy in John Steinbeck's Fiction." *The Moral Philosophy of John Steinbeck*. Edited by Stephen K. George. Lanham MD: Scarecrow Press, 2005: 41–48.

Hauser, Mark D. *Moral Minds: How Nature Designed Our Universal Sense of Right and Wrong*. New York: HarperCollins, 2006.

Heavilin, Barbara. "The Existential Vacuum and Ethan Hawley: John Steinbeck's Moral Philosophy." *The Moral Philosophy of John Steinbeck.* Edited by Stephen K. George. Lanham MD: Scarecrow Press, 2005: 49–58.

Hedgpeth, Joel. "John Steinbeck: Late-Blooming Environmentalist." *Steinbeck and the Environment*. Edited by Susan F. Beegel, Susan Shillinglaw, and Wesley N. H. Tiffney, Jr. Tuscaloosa: University of Alabama Press, 1997: 293–309.

———. "Philosophy on Cannery Row." *Steinbeck: The Man and His Work.* Edited by Richard Astro and Tetsumaro Hayashi. Corvallis: Oregon State University Press, 1971: 91–95.

Heidegger, Martin. *Being and Time*. Translated by John Macguarrie and Edward Robins. London: SCM Press, 1962.

Howells, William Dean. *Criticism and Fiction*. New York: Greenwood, 1977.

Hume, David. *Inquiry Concerning the Principles of Morals*. Edited by L. A. Selby-Brigge. Oxford: Oxford University Press, 1902, 1951.

Kelly, James C. "John Steinbeck and Ed Ricketts: Understanding Life in the Great Tide Pool." *Steinbeck and the Environment*. Edited by Susan F. Beegel, Susan Shillinglaw, and Wesley N. H. Tiffney, Jr. Tuscaloosa: University of Alabama Press, 1997: 27–42.

Kiernan, Thomas. *The Intricate Music: A Biography of John Steinbeck*. Boston: Little, Brown and Co., 1979

Kinney, Arthur F. "The Arthurian Cycle in *Tortilla Flat*." *Modern Fiction Studies* 11.1 (Spring 1965): 11–20.

Levant, Howard. *The Novels of John Steinbeck: A Critical Study*. Columbia: University of Missouri Press, 1974.

Lewis, C. S. *Miracles: A Preliminary Study*. New York: Macmillan, 1947, 1973.

Lisca, Peter. *John Steinbeck: Nature and Myth*. New York: Thomas Y. Crowell, 1978.

———. *The Wide World of John Steinbeck*. Brunswick: Rutgers University Press, 1958.

Lumiansky, R. M. *Morte D'Arthur*. New York: Macmillan, 1982.

Matthews, William. "Sin and Punishment in the Alliterative *Morte Arthur*." *Arthur King of Britain*. Edited by Richard L. Brengle. New York: Appleton-Century-Crofts, 1964: 379–391.

McFall, Lynne. "Integrity." *Ethics* 98.1 (October 1987): 5–20.

Melville, Herman. *Billy Budd, Sailor*. Edited by Milton R. Stern. Indianapolis: Bobbs-Merrill, 1975.

Morris, Harry. "*The Pearl*: Realism and Allegory." *English Journal* 52 (October 1963): 487–95, 503.

Oakley, Justin. *Morality and the Emotions*. New York: Routledge, 1993.

———. *Virtue Ethics and Professional Roles*. Cambridge: Cambridge University Press, 2006.

Pettit, Philip. "The Consequentialist Perspective." *Three Methods of Ethics: A Debute*. With Marcia W. Baron and Michael Slote. Malden MA: Blackwell Publishing, 1997.

Plantinga, Cornelius Jr. *Not the Way It's Supposed to Be: A Breviary of Sin*. Grand Rapids: Wm. B. Eerdmans, 1995.

Railsback, Brian. "Searching for 'What Is': Charles Darwin and John Steinbeck." *Steinbeck and the Environment*. Edited by Susan F. Beegel, Susan Shillinglaw, and Wesley N. H. Tiffney, Jr. Tuscaloosa: University of Alabama Press, 1997: 127–41.

Rawls, John. *A Theory of Justice*. Cambridge: Belknap Press of Harvard University, 1971.

Rosenberry, Edward H. "The Problem of *Billy Budd*." *PMLA* 80.5 (December 1965): 489–98.

Ross. W. D. *The Right and the Good*. Oxford: Oxford University Press, 1930.

Ross, Woodburn O. "John Steinbeck: Naturalism's Priest." *College English* 10.8 (May 1949): 433–39.

Sartre, Jean-Paul. *Being and Nothingness*. Translated by Hazel E. Barnes. New York: Philosophical Library, 1956.

———. *Nausea*. Translated by Lloyd Alexander. New York: New Dimension Press, 1964.

Schimmel, Solomon. *The Seven Deadly Sins: Jewish, Christian, and Classical Reflections on Human Nature*. New York: Macmillan, 1992.

Simmonds, Roy S. "The Unrealized Dream: Steinbeck's Modern Version of Malory." *Steinbeck and the Arthurian Theme*. Edited by Tetsumaro Hayashi. Steinbeck Monograph Series No. 5. Muncie: Ball State University, 1975.

Smuts, Jan Christian. *Holism and Evolution*. New York: Macmillan, 1926.

Stob, Henry. *Ethical Reflections: Essays on Moral Themes*. Grand Rapids: Wm. B. Eerdmans, 1978.

Stout, Jeffrey. *Ethics After Babel: The Languages of Morals and Their Discontents*. Princeton: Princeton University Press, 2001.

Sundermeier, Michael. "Why Steinbeck Didn't Finish His Arthur—*The Acts of King Arthur and His Noble Knights*." *Steinbeck's Posthumous Work: Essays in Criticism*. Edited by Tetsumaro Hayashi and Thomas J. Moore. Steinbeck Monograph Series No. 14. Muncie: Ball State University, 1989: 34–42.

Timmerman, John H. "The Shadow and *The Pearl*: Jungian Patterns in *The Pearl*." *The Short Novels of John Steinbeck*. Edited by Jackson J. Benson. Durham: Duke University Press, 1990: 143–61.

Walhout, Clarence. "The End of Literature." *Christianity and Literature* 47.4 (Summer 1998): 459–76.

Wilson, James Q. *The Moral Sense*. New York: Macmillan Free Press, 1993.

Wright, Nathalia. *Melville's Use of the Bible*. Durham: Duke University Press, 1949.

Index